SLUG
BREAD
&
BEHEADED
THISTLES

Amusing &
Useful
Techniques for
Nontoxic
Housekeeping
& Gardening

face no detrimentum

face no detrimentum

SLUG BREAD & BEHEADED THISTLES

ELLEN SANDBECK

Broadway Books • New York

BROADWAY

PRINTED IN THE UNITED STATES OF AMERICA

BROADWAY BOOKS and its logo, a letter B bisected on the diagonal, are trademarks of Broadway Books, a division of Random House, Inc.

Visit our website at www.broadwaybooks.com

First Broadway Books trade paperback edition published 2000, second edition published 2003.

Book design by Bonni Leon-Berman
Illustrations courtesy of Ellen Sandbeck

The Library of Congress has cataloged the first Broadway Books edition as follows:

Sandbeck, Ellen.
    Slug bread & beheaded thistles: amusing & useful techniques for nontoxic housekeeping & gardening / Ellen Sandbeck.
        p.   cm.
    Originally published: Duluth, MN: De la Terre Press, 1995.
    Includes bibliographical references and index.
    1. Household pests—Control.   2. Garden pests—Control.   I. Title: Slug bread & beheaded thistles.   II. Title.
TX325.S26   2000
648'.7—dc21   99-055147

ISBN 0-7679-0542-3

10 9 8 7

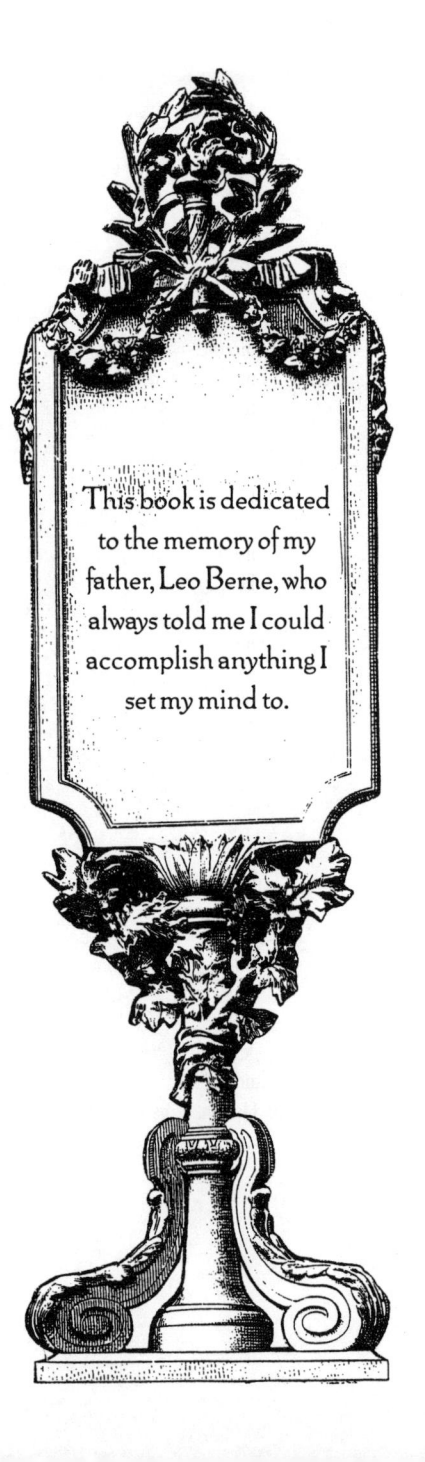

This book is dedicated to the memory of my father, Leo Berne, who always told me I could accomplish anything I set my mind to.

ACKNOWLEDGMENTS

I would like to thank the following people who helped facilitate this book:

My husband, Walter, stuff of life, staff of life

Dmitri and Ariadne Sandbeck, for research assistance

Ann Klefstad for editing and encouragement; Susie Newman for reusing everything in such a fun and stylish way; Grace Miller, our adopted grandmother and perfect role model; Liz Sarabia, greenhouse whiz; Eleanor, Charlie and Jim Nichol, gardening angels; Al, Lynda, Joseph and Freddie Parella, more gardening angels; and Jule Gagnon, Deer Goddess

Kind friends who make life worth living

Janis Donnaud, my agent, who encouraged me to expand the book, then edited it exquisitely

The heroic reference librarians at the Duluth Public Library, who always find what I need, and never flinch no matter how odd my topic

Thank you all!

CONTENTS

HOW TO USE THIS BOOK

THIS BOOK IS ORGANIZED around the idea of using and reusing materials as a way to help keep our environment and ourselves healthy. Using things more than once is also a good way to save money.

The sections of the book are organized (if anything that comes out of my mind can be called organized) around the pests, helpers, materials, and methods used to clean houses and eradicate pests. So, for instance, if you have a lot of coffee grounds, and you are wondering if there is anything amusing that can be done with them, look up coffee in the Index, where various uses for coffee grounds are all given in one place. If, on the other hand, you are seeking a way to remove cigarette smoke from a couch, look up cigarette smoke, removing, in the Index, and you will find another use for your old coffee grounds.

SLUG
BREAD
&
BEHEADED
THISTLES

INTRODUCTION

THE DEADLY SERIOUS APPROACH
to "pest" control is proving to be a deadly
mistake. Over one million human beings
are poisoned by pesticides each
year; twenty thousand of the
poisonings are fatal. Pesticides
are the leading cause of work-
related deaths in some Latin Ameri-
can countries. Indirect costs of pesticide use in
the United States are also very high; estimated
costs per year are: pesticide poisonings and related illnesses, $250 million; damage to agri-
cultural systems, $525 million; testing drink-
ing water for contamination, $1.3 billion;
destruction of fish and wildlife, $15 million;
livestock poisoning and contamination of meat and milk, $15
million.

David Pimental, professor of entomology at Cornell University, estimates that if we stopped all chemical pesticide use
overnight, crop losses to pests would increase by only 9 percent.
"Clearly," Pimental says, "the nation would not starve."

Insects are deadly serious, and they are beating us at our own
humorless game. Before World War II only seven species of insects were known to be resistant to chemical pesticides, now
over six hundred species of plant and animal pests are known to
be resistant as a result of exposure to pesticides. Despite a 33
percent increase in pesticide use since the 1940s, crop losses due
to pests have increased by 6 percent.

In contrast to what is happening to the insects, a 1987

National Cancer Institute study showed that in households where home or garden pesticides are used, children are up to six times more likely to develop leukemia than are children in non-pesticide homes. And a study published in the *Journal of the American Medical Association* showed that in 1990, deaths due to toxic pollutants and contaminants equaled the number of gunshot and motor vehicle fatalities combined. (In that year there were 60,000 deaths due to environmental pollutants; 35,000 due to firearms, and 25,000 as a result of motor vehicle accidents.)

Some man-made chemicals have been found to act as "hormone disrupters," or a sort of chemical saboteur. Hormone disrupters include the 209 PCBs, the 75 dioxins, and the 135 furans. These chemicals target and disrupt the chemical message system of the body by attacking natural hormones, scrambling or jamming messages or spreading disinformation. The body simply cannot tell the difference between the hormone mimic and the real thing.

The first recognized hormone disrupter was DDT, which was developed and put on the market in 1938.

In 1950, a young scientist discovered that exposure to DDT feminized young roosters. They never strutted, never learned to crow, didn't develop proper wattles or combs. No one paid any attention to this information, and DDT remained unrestricted on the U.S. market until 1972. By then, the bald eagle, our national symbol, had almost become extinct because of DDT-induced eggshell thinning.

Many hormonally active synthetic chemicals don't degrade readily into benign components. Many will be in the environment for a long time: for decades, even for centuries after they were first released.

We need a new attitude if we are to excel in the "human versus pests" game; we need to recover our sense of humor and realize that a worm in an apple is not life-threatening, and that nobody ever died of having dandelions in a lawn. We need all the

laughs we can get in our dealings with pests, or we will be deadly serious all the way to the cemetery. In 1931, before the advent of big chemical farming, archie the cockroach wrote, with a little help from his friend Don Marquis, in his book *archie and mehitabel:* "i will admit that some/of the insects do not lead/noble lives but is every/mans hand to be against them/yours for less justice/and more charity archie."

If we do not begin to show more charity toward the earth and her natural systems, the insect, plant, and animal pests really will inherit the earth; they are a lot tougher than we are. In fact, rats are so wildly fertile that chemically exposed male rats whose sperm levels have dropped to 5 percent of normal can still easily father babies. This is not the case with humans, who have naturally rather low sperm counts, which, as a matter of fact, have been dropping precipitously since the advent of the chemical age.

We human beings are an inventive and humorous species; only our sense of humor can save us from the dreadful predicament we have gotten ourselves into. Here is my contribution to the cause: pest control with a giggle (or perhaps it's a smirk).

GARDENING

IN 1991, THE ENVIRONMENTAL PROTECTION AGENCY (EPA) completed a five-year study, *The National Survey of Pesticides in Drinking Water Wells;* more than half of the 94,000 drinking water wells in the United States contained nitrates from fertilizers; 10 percent of the community wells and 4 percent of the rural wells contained pesticides. The most commonly detected pesticide was Dacthal, an herbicide used on lawns!

Suburban homeowners use more pesticides per acre than farmers do: $1 billion is spent on home pesticides annually at great cost to environmental and human health. Insects and diseases are more likely to attack plants and animals that are weakened through environmental or chemical stress; they stalk the least fit plants in the field or garden, just as predators attack the slowest, weakest members of an animal herd.

Though my husband and I landscaped professionally using only organic methods for years, I have not had the opportunity to try all of the pest control methods I am including in this chapter. We have simply never had many pests to deal with. Having healthy organic soil and choosing only plants that are fully hardy in your climate zone seem to preclude huge infestations of insect pests; and keeping the soil well covered with mulch or ground cover prevents erosion while lowering the weed population. I have tried to be very careful about including only methods that have been well documented, if I have not been able to test them myself.

"PESTS" ARE PESTS because they are prolific opportunists: human activities are making the world more habitable for pest species, while damaging more delicate organisms.

"Weeds" are nature's front-line defense against bare ground, and they are well equipped for the job. Some weeds have defensive weapons such as thorns, glue, or poison.

All weeds have amazing reproductive capabilities and brilliant deployment methods: stickery hitchhiking seeds (Velcro was first invented by burdocks), parachuting seeds, seeds that shoot, seeds that screw themselves into the ground, seeds that digest insects, seeds that can wait like Sleeping Beauty for hundreds of years for the right time to awaken and grow, and plants that spring back to life in greater numbers after being chopped to pieces.

Dear, we may be having a baby.

Weeds have to be tough. They have important work to do protecting the earth from devastating erosion. Unfortunately, the important work weeds do goes largely unappreciated by gardeners who have thistles in their rose beds, dandelions in their lawns, burdock seeds in their dogs' fur, and poison ivy rashes.

Chemical herbicides

A 1993 report from the National Academy of Sciences found sufficient evidence to link exposure to dioxin-contaminated herbicides to three cancers: soft-tissue sarcoma, non-Hodgkin's lymphoma, and Hodgkin's disease. Dioxins are formed during the herbicide manufacturing process, and they are present in all chemical herbicides.

Just in times

In 1982 and 1983, Times Beach, Missouri, was evacuated by the U.S. government. Dioxin-contaminated waste oil had been sprayed on the roads to keep down the dust.

Children who were born after the evacuation had damaged immune systems and brain damage that shortened their attention spans as well as their tempers.

Rotting teeth

Dental researchers in Helsinki, Finland, turned up a connection in 1999 between young children whose new molars are malformed, discolored, and decay easily, and exposure to high levels of dioxins in their mothers' breast milk.

LAWNS

The harder we try for the perfect single species lawn, the more insect infestations we have, and the weaker the lawn. Lawns are terrific energy wasters in the U.S. In order to keep up with the Joneses, Americans use gas-hogging lawnmowers, which emit far more pollution than do cars, to cut the lawns they have just fertilized into growing faster with fertilizer made of nonrenewable petroleum products. The EPA estimates that running a gas mower for one hour generates as much air pollution as running a car for almost two days! In 1999, as of this writing, the EPA is finally starting to implement emission standards for small engines of 25 hp or less, like those found in lawn and garden equipment.

In order to cut down on your lawn's energy use, as well as on air and noise pollution, cut your lawn with a push mower if possible, or at least get an electric mower. Plant white Dutch clover in with the grass (clover is a legume that fixes nitrogen in the soil); set the mower blades as high as possible so that weeds get shaded out; leave the grass clippings on the lawn where they can break down and release nutrients into the soil; and when you pull weeds, sprinkle grass and clover seeds in the bare spots. Water in the early morning or evening to cut down on evaporation.

THE PRIMAVERA LAWN CORSET

When you take care of your lawn in an environmentally sound way, you will be rewarded with a thriving earthworm population. Earthworms cannot live in a chemically contaminated environment, and earthworms are a lawn's best friends; they help keep a lawn well aerated, and each earthworm produces $\frac{1}{3}$ pound of high-quality fertilizer per year. It is a real pleasure watching the early bird hunting worms on your lawn, knowing that it will not become an avian poisoning victim.

If your lawn is way too big for a push mower, and you are not a groundskeeper for a ball team, maybe you should consider reducing the size of your lawn.

There are some types of grass, such as buffalo grass, which are low growing and don't really require mowing, unless you are growing a putting green. Check into what types of short grasses will work in your area or, better yet, plant a meadow and learn to identify butterflies.

Scientists in the Netherlands reported in 1999 that the cut ends of freshly mown grass release volatile organic compounds

(VOCs) that form smog. So kick back and relax in your hammock. "Sorry dear, I can't mow the lawn, I'm busy fighting global warming."

EXORCISING WEEDS

Because weeds evolved to colonize bare soil, fertile soil is relatively weed resistant. So the first line of defense against weeds is to build up the soil with organic matter. The second thing to do,

especially in perennial beds, is to lay down a thick layer of mulch made of an organic material (straw, leaves, shredded bark) to prevent weed seeds from reaching the ground.

Lastly, remember that many weed seeds can remain dormant for decades buried under the ground, and deep tilling can bring these "sleepers" to the surface, where they can germinate, producing weeds you may never have seen before.

So let sleeping weeds lie. Just cover them with a deeper blanket of mulch.

Wounded grasses strike back

When injured or killed, winter rye, sorghum, Sudan grass, and winter barley all release chemicals that are toxic to young seedlings. Plant any of these grasses, mow, and use the grass clippings as a source of weed suppressant mulch.

Let them eat cabbage!

In the fall, try blending cabbage leaves in the blender with some water and pouring the resultant mush in the cracks of your sidewalk, in your perennial beds, or anywhere else to prevent weeds from germinating in the spring.

Bernard Bible, a professor at the University of Connecticut, found that cruciferous plants (cabbage, broccoli, kale, Brussels sprouts, etc.) contain thiocyanate, a chemical that is toxic to newly germinated plants, especially those with small seeds. Mild-tasting crucifers like cabbage have the highest levels of thiocyanate. Brussels sprouts are reported to have the highest thiocyanate levels of all, and I am hoping that now I will have a good excuse for not eating them: "I'm sorry, I need to pour these Brussels sprouts in the cracks in my sidewalk, I can't possibly eat them!"

Drunken weeds

Spray individual weeds with isopropyl alcohol or full-strength vinegar on a sunny day to kill them. Pour vinegar or isopropyl alcohol on weeds growing in sidewalk cracks.

Get a grip

Using pliers enables a gardener to pull out really tough weeds.

When I was a little girl, I used pliers to pull seedling plums up out of our ivy. When I tried pulling them out without pliers, the seedlings always broke off at ground level; the resprouted seedlings were even tougher the next time I weeded.

Poison Ivy and Poison Oak

These botanical bullies present such uniquely difficult problems that I am going to devote quite a bit of space to them.

Battlegear

When battling your poison ivy, poison sumac, or poison oak patch, always wear appropriate attire: long pants, long-sleeved shirt, hat, goggles, rubber gloves, and rubber boots.

Dig down to expose the plants' roots so you can pour boiling water on them. Flood the roots with boiling water, then smother the plants with black or clear plastic sheeting, weight the plastic down on the edges with rocks and dirt, and leave the plastic on all summer.

Never, never burn any part of a poison oak, sumac, or ivy plant. The smoke disperses the irritating oils widely, and inhaling the smoke can be extremely dangerous.

After you are done with your eradication project, wash all your clothing in hot water and detergent and scrub your boots and goggles with hot water and detergent. Then take a hot shower and scrub yourself thoroughly. If it looks as if your eradication project will last more than a couple of hours, take a shower break every two hours or so to wash the plant oils off your skin. Be careful not to put clothing with the plant oils on it anywhere but in the washing machine! The oils rub off very easily.

The boiling water and plastic sheeting method can also be used on other extremely persistent perennial weeds like polygonum or ivy. You must be diligent about pouring boiling water on any new shoots that come up, however.

CREATING WEEDS

Some garden plants are like Frankenstein's monster: planted on purpose, they turn out to be too rampant to control. The worst weeds in the garden plant category tend to be perennials whose roots travel widely and send up shoots, like Lombardy poplar and bamboo in warm climates, or polygonum in cold climates; plants that crawl aboveground and send down roots, like ivy; and perennial plants that produce masses of seeds. Chopping up some of these plants only makes them spread more quickly, as all the chopped-up pieces grow into new plants. These "Frankenstein" plants can be a problem that affects much more than an individual garden. For example, purple loosestrife is an escaped garden plant which is threatening the balance of wetlands in many parts of the U.S. by crowding out native plants that provide food and shelter for wildlife. Avoid these colonizing pests by talking to experienced gardeners, who can tell you which plants are problems in your area.

"Good" weeds can be created if you plant small annuals or perennials that reproduce quickly by seeding but are easy to control. Some good examples of "nice" weeds are: alyssum, Johnny-jump-ups, forget-me-nots, poppies, and violets. They are all small, easy to pull out, and pretty. Bear in mind that weeds will colonize every square inch of bare soil in your garden unless the soil is poisoned beyond repair. Wouldn't you prefer to have alyssum growing in the cracks of your sidewalk rather than thistles? How about violets in your lawn instead of plantain? Experienced gardeners in your area

His lawn looked just like
green velvet!

should be able to recommend some garden plants that will fit the bill. They will probably even supply you with some!

USING WEEDS

Many weeds are very high in bioactive chemicals, which help protect them from insect and animal predation. USDA scientist James A. Duke suggests that the human body may have better tolerance for natural compounds than for man-made compounds: "Man's genes and immune system have been exposed to the natural compounds. They haven't been exposed to tomorrow's synthetic compounds." In fact, one quarter of all prescription drugs contain plant derivatives or synthetic copies of plant compounds.

The persistence of many of the man-made hormone mimics makes them even more dangerous: some of these synthetic chemicals can persist in the body for years, while plant estrogens might be broken down and eliminated within a day.

I am including only a few examples of my favorite uses for weeds. For more com-plete information on this extremely interesting and complex subject, please read some of the books on weeds listed in the Bibliography. Your local librarian can help you find more information as well.

Mustard on the side

Mustards and their kin will help clean up salty soils. (Plant alyssum in your salty roadside bed, or phlox, or flowering kale, or plain old mustards.)

Fatal attraction

Japanese beetles adore *Geranium maculatum,* a wild species-geranium with small pink flowers. They are irresistibly attracted to *Geranium maculatum,* eat it, and die!

Other types of geraniums act as Japanese beetle narcotics, knocking the beetles out for eight hours, and halving their reproductive rate.

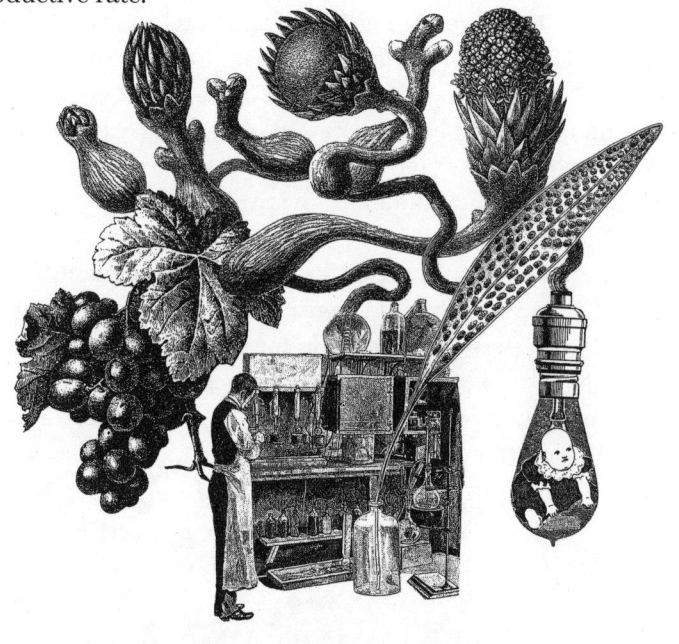

A kinder, gentler antifungal

Horsetail (equisetum) spray kills powdery mildew and other fungi. Boil a potful of fresh equisetum for fifteen to twenty minutes. Let the tea cool and use it as a spray against fungus and mildew on plants. It does not disturb the soil life, unlike more powerful antifungal sprays.

Equisetum growing is a sign that the soil is very wet. The way to get rid of equisetum is to build up the soil with compost and improve the drainage.

Horsetail should not be allowed to grow in pastures; it can poison livestock.

Blood curdling

Yarrow (*Achillea millefolium*) is a weed as well as a pretty garden perennial. The fresh or dried leaves and flowers act as a styptic. A snuff made of dried yarrow is very effective at staunching nosebleeds. Gardeners used to wind yarrow around their tool handles to use in case of emergencies. (Yarrow will not take the place of a tourniquet. If you have an accident with your chainsaw, call 911!) Yarrow is effective only for minor gardening injuries like cuts and scrapes.

Sap curdling

Aloe vera gel or juice may be used to cover a tree wound after pruning. The surface will heal over quickly, and insects are repelled by the bitter aloe taste. Aloe can also be used as a rabbit repellent.

Body building

Stinging nettles are extremely nutritious and strengthening for plants and animals. Fresh nettles have a nasty sting, caused by the fine hairs on the leaves and stems. Wear gloves or put plastic bags over your hands when you go nettle gathering.

Cooked or dried nettles no longer sting. Once you have tasted nettles, you will go gathering frequently: nettle tea is deliciously meaty tasting, and young nettles make a fine addition to soups.

Nettles are wonderful in compost piles too, but we prefer to eat our nettles instead.

Compost building

Thistles are rich in potassium, and should be composted, well buried, in the middle of the pile.

If you can't lick 'em, compost 'em

Water hyacinth (*Eichhornia crassipes*), is a beautiful little tropical American water plant. It has escaped from cultivation and covered many waterways in warm parts of the United States. Manatees love to eat it, but boaters hate it because it clogs their propellers.

Do yourself and your waterway a favor: bring a load of water hyacinth home with you and compost it. DO NOT LET ANY WATER HYACINTH DROP INTO WATERWAYS ON YOUR WAY HOME!

Slime thyme

Green pond algae, also known as scum or slime, makes a really good fertilizer. Scoop some up and top-dress your garden with it.

SOIL AND WATER

Soil and water are completely intertwined; when one is poisoned, so is the other.

IS YOUR SOIL A NINETY-POUND WEAKLING? BUILD IT UP!

We lose over six billion tons of topsoil annually in the U.S. This is the equivalent of losing 1 inch of soil off all the farmland in Maine, New Hampshire, Vermont, New York, New Jersey, Pennsylvania, Delaware, Maryland, Alabama, Arizona, California, and Florida.

Human beings cannot survive on a diet of vitamin pills alone, and soil cannot survive on chemicals alone. It is time to start building our soil back up with a healthful diet of manures, mulches, and compost.

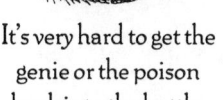

It's very hard to get the genie or the poison back into the bottle.

There's a fungus among us

If we are trees, we can't thrive without our "pet" fungus. Fungi grow into the roots of all conifers and many other forest trees. Photosynthesizing trees capture carbon dioxide and convert it into sugars. The trees trade sugars to the fungi in exchange for phosphorus. The fungi scavenge phosphorus from the soil, making it more available to the trees. Since phosphorus can be difficult for plants to obtain, the tree and the fungus both benefit from their symbiotic relationship.

To each according to his needs, from each according to his capabilities

Researchers from the Ministry of Forests in Kamloops, British Columbia, found that some trees share carbon with their neighbors. An underground network of fungal filaments (called mycorrhiza) envelops the roots of different tree species, connecting forest trees to each other and delivering carbon from one tree to another. Trees growing in the shade receive extra carbon, trees growing in the sun give more carbon.

Throw a handful of good rich forest soil into your tree's planting hole, in order to make sure the tree has the mychorrizae it needs, or buy mycorrhizal inoculant. If you

Yes.

have a young tree that isn't thriving, take some soil from around the base of a healthy tree of the same species, and work the healthy soil in around the ailing sapling.

The fungus is like us

The pyrimidine carbinol family of fungicides kill fungi by inhibiting the production of fatty compounds called sterols. Sterols are necessary to form the fungus's cell walls.

These fungicides also inhibit mammals' ability to produce steroids. Steroid hormones are responsible for determining our gender.

I'd rather live with a little mold and mildew than be an "it"; thanks anyway.

FEED YOUR SOIL A HEALTHY DIET OR PAY THE PRICE

Inorganic fertilizers cause vegetables to be much higher in nitrates than organically grown vegetables. Remember the scare about nitrosamines in hot dogs causing cancer? Chemically grown beets, spinach, celery, and lettuce all have higher nitrate levels than do processed meats!

Inorganically grown produce may not be so good for humans, but it is wonderful for insect pests. According to a study done by Miguel A. Altieri, Ph.D., and his colleagues at the University of California at Berkeley, test plots of organically fertilized broccoli outproduced plots of chemically fertilized broccoli. The organically grown broccoli attracted fewer insect pests than the chemically fertilized broccoli did. Dr. Altieri's broccoli thrived on 7 to 8 gallons of compost per 100 square feet.

Dr. Altieri explains that many pest insects are attracted to high nitrogen levels in plant leaves. There is more available nitrogen in chemically fertilized leaves than in organically grown leaves.

Don't drink the water

You don't even have to eat produce to ingest too many nitrates from fertilizers. Many rural water supplies are heavily contaminated by nitrate-laden runoff from fields; blue babies are the result. Blue babies have a bluish skin tint because of inadequate levels of oxygen in their blood due to heart or blood vessel defects.

Don't eat the fish

Great Lakes fish are heavily contaminated with PCBs and other chemical pollutants that are very resistant to breakdown, and bioaccumulate in body fat. A 1980s study of mothers who ate a lot of fish from the Great Lakes showed that they had lower-birth-weight babies with smaller head circumferences and weaker reflexes than those of mothers who ate no fish. At age four, the fish-eating mothers' children had lower verbal and memory test scores.

In a parallel study, adult rats were fed salmon from Lake Ontario. When life was easy, the fish-fed rats seemed normal. But the fish-eating rats were "hyperreactive" to even mildly negative situations. Under the same conditions, the nonfish-eating control rats kept their cool.

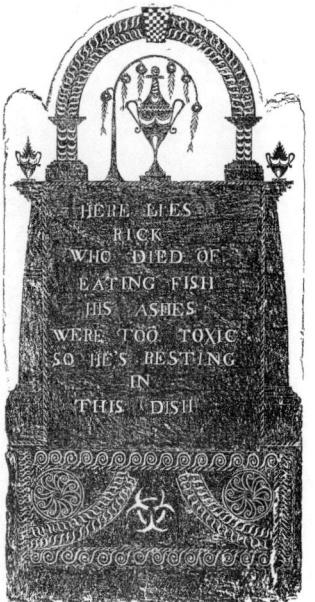

These behavioral changes were passed along to the rats' children and grandchildren. Only the first generation of rats in the study was fed contaminated salmon; all subsequent generations were fed rat chow. The PCBs were being passed from the mother rats to their offspring during gestation and lactation.

> ## Please! Don't Wave That Thing Around!
> *Researchers at the University of Wisconsin at Madison provided lab rats and mice with drinking water containing the same levels of pesticide and fertilizer contamination as were found in wells in rural Dane County, Wisconsin. The well-water rats exhibited unpredictable bursts of aggression. The clean-water rodents had no bursts of aggression.*
>
> *Could prenatal exposure to contaminants be reducing our ability to cope with stress? Were our grandparents shooting each other on the highways over fender benders?*

Don't swim there

Vast growths, or "blooms," of blue-green algae, which can produce deadly toxins, have been increasing worldwide since the 1970s, poisoning an increasing number of people and wildlife. Scientists believe that the algal blooms are caused by nutrient-rich runoff due to deforestation, erosion, and overfertilization.

He must have drunk the water.

Water is far too precious a substance to waste. The big drought in California in the 1970s came close to splitting the state along north/south lines.

Clean water is one of our four most precious resources, along with clean air, clean soil, and healthy children.

I Think I'll Pass on the Clam Chowder

There is a growing incidence of tumors in East Coast shellfish. Jan H. Landsberg, of the Florida Marine Research Institute in Saint Petersburg, layered maps of algal blooms over regions with high numbers of shellfish tumors, and correlated the dates of blooms to reports of tumors. She said, "I found a very compelling picture. You see that high rates [of shellfish tumors] cluster very strongly with the incidence of algal blooms." She found that certain algal toxins stimulate cancer growth in mice.

Says Sylvia A. Earle, the National Geographic Society's explorer-in-residence, "The biosphere—the place where life occurs—is 95 percent ocean. So if the oceans are in trouble, so are we. And the oceans are in trouble." With research and stronger pollution controls, she adds, "that needn't remain the case."

Go native

If you have just moved to Arizona from Minnesota, please don't plant paper birches and a big lawn to make yourself feel at home. You will be wasting water as well as adding unnecessary humidity to the normally arid Arizona climate.

Plant native plants and mulch them to conserve water no matter where you live.

Don't be a water hog

Clean your sidewalks with a broom, not with a hose.

SECONDHAND WATER FOR YOUR SECONDHAND ROSE

Old dishwater

Use dish soap instead of dish detergent, and throw the old dishwater on your outdoor plants. Dish soap is healthier for you as well as for your plants.

The beer garden

After you wash out returnable or recyclable beer bottles, water your plants with the beery water.

Garden party

Water acid-lovers like azaleas, rhododendrons, and strawberries with cold tea or coffee.

Unfizzy water

Water plants with the water from boiling eggs, or with club soda that has lost its fizz.

AND DON'T BREATHE THE AIR

Increased nitrogen in the soil, caused by overfertilization, could be causing a buildup of methane in the atmosphere.

I could not resist the following, even though I realize that some of you do not own cows:

How to deflate a cow

To relieve a cow of bloat caused by overly rich food (bloat can kill a cow quickly), mix 1 tablespoon nonadditive, unscented detergent with 1 quart water. Pour the detergent water

down the cow's throat. The detergent breaks up the surface tension of the gas bubbles in the cow's stomach so the gas can be belched out. (Cow belches, of course, add to global warming by putting more methane into the air; it's all the cows' fault.)

Use the detergent cure only in an emergency!

SOIL BUILDING

Many soil amendments are mined, even some of the organic ones. Mining causes environmental damage, so try to produce your own fertilizers as much as possible. If you do buy soil amendments, select only products that are made of renewable resources: for example, manure, crop residues, seaweed, blood meal, bonemeal, shredded wood, or bark.

For most gardens, however, composting, mulching, bringing animal manures home, and growing green manures should be adequate.

MULCH! MULCH! MULCH!

Mulches discourage diseases and pests and help prevent erosion. Use shredded leaves, dry grass clippings, pine needles, straw, or whatever plant materials without pesticides you can find and legally bring home. Lake Superior produces a truly wonderful, dark, finely shredded mulch made out of driftwood that has been pulverized on the lake's rocks. We bring it home in bags whenever we find piles of it on the shore.

Mulch cool-weather crops early in the season to keep the soil cool; mulch warm-weather crops after the soil has warmed up. Keep mulches away from the trunks of trees and the crowns of perennials to prevent rodent damage and rot, respectively.

Pest jawbreaker

A layer of crushed limestone built up around tree trunks helps prevent rodents from chewing on tree roots.

Sawdust berries

A sawdust mulch around your strawberry plants will help prevent slug damage. Use sawdust from untreated wood only, please.

Needled

Pine needle mulch around plant containers helps keep slugs down. Strawberries also adore a pine needle mulch because of its acidity.

MANURE

Here is what E. B. White had to say about manure in *One Man's Meat:* "There is no doubt about it, the basic satisfaction in farming is manure, which always suggests that life can be cyclic and chemically perfect and aromatic and continuous." How could I possibly add to that?

Free fertilizer

If you have access to some well-composted, chemical-free horse, cow, chicken, or sheep manure, take as much as you can home with you. Use it liberally all over your garden. Do not bother to till it in; if it is left on top of the soil, it will attract earthworms and its nutrients will be more accessible to plants. Make sure you are getting well-composted manure; "new" manure may be too "hot" as well as full of viable weed seeds, and uncomposted chicken manure could make you extremely unpopular with your neighbors.

COMPOST

Compost your food waste! Save the world!

Food refuse, because of its high moisture content, is the least desirable component of garbage being burned in incinerators. Garbage incinerators burn cooler because of wet food wastes. Dioxins are produced when chlorine-containing compounds such as plastic are burned at the lower temperatures.

Food wastes are also the least stable component in landfills, as well as the most likely source of leachate. Leachate can move toxic chemicals into surface and/or groundwater.

Incidentally, the compost pile should not be directly adjacent to the vegetable garden, because many of its denizen decomposers—for instance, slugs, snails, sow bugs, pill bugs, and earwigs—are not so good for the garden.

Don't touch that pile!

Tests conducted on large-scale compost piles in Quebec and Pennsylvania showed that unturned compost piles contain up to 13 percent more nitrogen than is found in compost piles turned twice a week.

More nitrogen escapes as ammonia gas when compost piles

are turned frequently. If the pile isn't turned, microbes can convert the ammonia into a more stable form of nitrogen.

I am not a talented outdoor composter. One year, after spring cleanup, I looked up at the top of my compost pile and realized that it was not working, and had probably not been for several years. There was no more room on top of the pile. So I industriously turned and watered it for a month. It was unrepentant, and continued to sneer down at me. In desperation, I threw in a few thousand red wriggler worms from my indoor composting bin. Within a week, the pile had dropped a couple of feet.

Now I add more red wrigglers each spring, then sit back and watch my compost pile shrink while the worms do all the work.

Easy does it

Research by Safer Agro-Chem of Victoria, British Columbia, has shown that compost produces fatty acids that are toxic to pathogenic fungi and bacterial diseases of plants. They found that compost made the "lazy," passive, low-temperature way was best at suppressing disease! The Lazy Way may be the best way, something I have long suspected.

It's a gas

Soils high in organic matter and nitrogen produce more ethylene than do infertile soils; ethylene gas discourages the growth of fungus.

Give 'em a shot in the limb

Composting residues from diseased plants may help plants build up immunity to disease. For example: the ancient Romans used to compost black rot–infected grapes, then use the finished compost as a mulch around their grapevines, because they knew the practice helped the vines resist the disease. Mulch "inoculations" against plant diseases work in the same way as vaccinations do for mammals: they activate the organism's immune system.

Throw all your leaves, soft clippings, pulled weeds, and vegetable residues in your compost pile and leave it alone. If your neighbor brags about how hot his compost pile is, explain to him that cool compost has been scientifically proven to be a superior product, then go lounge in a hammock somewhere and listen to a ball game.

Plan to use your pile of antibiotic compost next year.

Mineral supplements

Hair, human or animal, is very good for the garden; it is full of valuable trace minerals that keep plants happy. Throw the hair you have cleaned out of your hairbrush, and Fido's shed winter coat in your compost pile.

Don't be inhibited

Keep walnut leaves out of your compost pile. Walnut leaves inhibit the growth of everything!

Get the lead out

If you are worried about high lead levels in your yard from old paint chips or car exhaust, cover the soil with a huge amount of compost.

Research done at Cornell University's Urban Horticultural Institute shows that soils with very high amounts of organic matter in them, and a neutral pH (6.5 to 7), will prevent plants from taking up lead and cadmium, even if the lead levels are very high (up to 3,000 ppm). Very well-composted material works better than uncomposted mulch.

Molasses, breakfast of champions

In 1996, researchers at the Joliet (Illinois) Army Ammunition Plant recruited bacteria to clean up twelve thousand pounds of soil that had been contaminated with weapons-grade TNT.

The scientists added a few kilograms of molasses weekly to 300-gallon batches of contaminated soil and water. Within weeks, the TNT levels dropped from 7,000 mg TNT per kilogram of soil to 20 mg TNT per kilogram of soil.

Unrefined, agricultural molasses makes a perfect bacteria chow, supplying lots of sugars, proteins, and amino acids that growing bacteria need. "Explosives are tougher compounds to degrade than others," said Mark L. Hampton, of the Army Environmental Center in Aberdeen, Maryland, so the technique would probably work for other contaminants, including chlorinated solvents, wood-preserving chemicals, and petroleum.

Do your bacteria a favor: fill a watering can with molasses water, and water down your compost!

GARDEN PESTS

Bugs have eaten half the leaves off your squash plant? Deer are eating your beans? Don't worry, be happy!

A study done by Michael Hoffman, of Cornell University, demonstrated that many plants stayed healthy and produced normally even after many of their leaves had been removed or stripped. Bean plants stayed healthy until more than 50 percent of their leaves were gone; winter squash shrugged off up to 60 percent defoliation; and young pumpkin plants showed no reduction in yields until more than 80 percent of their leaves were removed.

Plants need to be kept well watered after they have lost a lot of leaves, however.

TRAPPING AND REPELLING GARDEN PESTS

Hot they don't got

Habanero peppers will repel everything, from ants to zebra mussels!

Entomologist Dr. Geoff Zehnder, of Auburn University in Alabama, tested the plant-protecting efficiency of red pepper extract, *Bacillus thuringiensis* (Bt), and lambda-cyhalothrin (a chemical insecticide).

Two years of testing proved that Bt and hot red pepper were each

better than the chemical insecticide at protecting cabbage plants from cabbage loopers, diamondback moth larvae, and imported cabbage worms.

Dr. Zehnder's hot recipe:

2 tablespoons McCormick Hot Red Pepper and 6 drops liquid dish soap, dissolved in 1 gallon water. Stir the solution and spray your plants with it weekly.

Roly-poly trap

Make a sow-bug and pill-bug trap by cutting the top off a 2-liter soda pop bottle, and inverting the top onto the rest of the bottle, which is now cylindrical. Tape the joint. Bait the trap with dog food. Sow bugs and pill bugs will get in and not out. Release the prisoners in the compost heap; these tiny crustaceans are decomposers.

One potato, two potato, wireworms no more

Wireworms are the larvae of click beetles. Bait wireworms with pieces of potato, cut side down on the ground. Pick up the potato a couple of times a week, and destroy it along with the wireworms.

Tar and ashes

Repel root maggot flies by sprinkling wood ashes liberally around the stems of seedlings (cabbage, carrot, turnip, onion, corn). The adult fly lays her eggs on the roots of seedlings. Replace the ashes when they get soaked.

The traditional way to deter root maggot flies is to slip a small mat made of tar paper with a slit in it around the plant stem. Cover the slits with waterproof tape. The mats will prevent the maggots from penetrating the soil.

Walking on eggshells

Crushed eggshells repel root maggots and cutworms. Put a thin layer of crushed eggshells around the plant stems, then cover the eggshells with soil. The eggshells are uncomfortably sharp for the soft little insects to crawl through. Eggshells are also a good source of calcium for the soil.

EXTERIOR DECORATING

Variety is the spice of life

Plants in a monoculture are more susceptible to insect attack: insects find their food through chemical signals, and large groups of a single species create a strong chemical beacon.

The Japanese create bent and crooked garden paths because they believe that evil spirits travel in straight lines. They may be onto something: insects travel in straight lines. Long straight rows of a single plant species are just what the destructive insect ordered.

Psst! Want to buy a perfect apple?

The pests' fave

Yellow is many insect pests' favorite color. Aphids and small flies are irresistibly attracted to bright yellow. (Our children had a little yellow plastic chair, which the aphids thought was the bee's knees.)

There are two different types of yellow traps: yellow sticky traps, and yellow containers full of water. Commercial yellow sticky traps are made of stiff yellow paper covered with stickum. You can make your own sticky trap by putting a clear plastic bag over a yellow-painted can, then coating the bag with Tanglefoot (available in garden centers, hardware stores, and by mail order) or petroleum jelly. Put the can on a stake in the garden. When the bag is coated with insects, throw it away and replace it.

A yellow container filled with water will drown a lot of aphids. Half of a yellow plastic Easter egg filled with water makes a good aphid trap for houseplants.

Faux apple blossoms

Just before apple blossoms open, cover small sheets of white cardboard with Tree Tanglefoot, and hang them in your apple trees.

Female moths will mistake the white cardboard for apple blossoms, and try to lay their eggs on it. When the cardboard gets full of moths, throw it away and replace it. Keep trapping until all the blossoms have fallen.

Apple maggot preventer

Red spheres are a super-attractant for apple flies. Before the fruit ripens, smear Tanglefoot (available at garden centers, at hardware stores, and by mail order) on apple-sized balls and hang them in your apple trees. The female apple flies will try to lay eggs on the sticky traps.

Save yourself some messy cleaning chores by wrapping the spheres tightly in plastic bags and smearing the bags with Tanglefoot.

Placemats for melons

Put heavy waxed paper or waxed cardboard under melons to keep them from being invaded by worms.

OUTDOOR ENTERTAINING

COFFEE? TEA?

Give 'em the shakes

Don't throw out that old, cold coffee. Pour it on your un-invited insect guests.

When exposed to caf-feine, mosquito larvae get so uncoordinated they drown; tobacco budworms stop eat-ing, develop tremors, and die; and mealworms can't reproduce.

Dr. James A. Nathanson, neurologist at Harvard Medical School, found that concentrated doses of caffeine killed insects within hours or days. He used powdered coffee and tea.

Freshly brewed ants

Kill ants in lawns by pouring 1 pound coffee grounds in 1 quart boiling water over the anthill. A very big anthill may require a larger amount of coffee and hot water.

Disgust-a-maggot!

Sprinkle used tea leaves in your newly seeded vegetable garden to repel radish and turnip maggots. Fresh coffee grounds will repel carrot root maggots.

SUGAR?

Nematodes: kill 'em with sweetness

Boil ½ cup sugar in 2 cups water, stir until the sugar has completely dissolved. Let the sugar water cool, then dilute it with 1 gallon water. Spray the solution over your garden soil. The sugar will dry out and kill the nematodes.

Asparagus disgust

Nematodes hate asparagus. Pour your asparagus cooking water over tomato plants. Asparagus juice has been found to be effective at killing nematodes.

MILK?

Viruses hate milk

Skim milk spray kills tobacco mosaic virus, which can affect all members of the Solanaceae family (tobacco, tomatoes, eggplant, potatoes, peppers). Pickers in commercial pepper and tomato plots used to dip their hands in skim milk to prevent transmitting the mosaic virus from plant to plant.

Milk spray also kills other plant viruses. (Viruses often cause leaf mottling.)

This is a very good way to use up soured skim milk.

Sour worms

Sour milk or buttermilk can be sprinkled over cabbages to guard them against cabbage worms. The milky water from rinsing out returnable or recyclable milk jugs would be perfect for this.

GARLIC IS REALLY HEALTHY TOO

Seedling protection

To prevent downy and powdery mildew and to protect seedlings from damping off, boil 10 cloves garlic in 1 quart water for 30 minutes. Strain and let cool to room temperature. Use as a spray.

Strongly brewed chamomile tea also works well to prevent seedling damp-off.

Strawberry protection

Plant garlic with strawberries to repel insect pests.

Sulfur breath

One clove of garlic planted near roses helps repel aphids and greenflies.

The garlic also exudes sulfur, which will kill black spot fungus.

Insecticidal garlic spray

Soak 3 ounces finely minced garlic in 2 teaspoons mineral oil for 24 hours. Slowly add 1 pint water that has been mixed with $1/4$ ounce insecticidal soap. Stir thoroughly and strain into a glass jar for storage. Use 1 to 2 tablespoons per pint of water. Spray on insect-infested plants. If the spray causes leaf damage, dilute the solution more.

Rodale's All-Purpose Spray

Liquefy 1 garlic bulb and 1 small onion, add 1 teaspoon powdered cayenne pepper, and mix with 1 quart water. Let steep for 1 hour, strain through cheesecloth, then add 1 tablespoon liquid soap. Mix well and use.

Leave the soap out, and you can use this recipe to flavor your chili!

Odor removal

Onion and garlic odors can be removed by washing your hands thoroughly with cold water and soap. Hot water washes the odors into your skin.

CURE YOUR PLANTS' INDIGESTION

Out, out, black spot!

A 0.5 percent solution of baking soda (bicarbonate of soda) and water (3 teaspoons baking soda per gallon of water) sprayed on roses is a remedy for black spot and powdery mildew. (Based on research by R. K. Horst, professor of plant pathology at Cornell University)

Put out the fire blight

To cure fire blight, a bacterial infection that causes tree branches to look black and burned, spray the infected tree, especially the afflicted area, with a water and vinegar solution: 4 parts vinegar to 6 parts water. Spray again two weeks later.

SOAP SPRAYS

Soap sprays are highly effective at killing soft-bodied insects like aphids, scale, and whiteflies. Use the least perfumed dish soap or liquid household soap you can find, or buy Safer's Insecticidal Soap. The Safer's soap is formulated so it doesn't make suds.

1. Follow directions on the insecticidal soap label, or use a 1½ to 2 percent solution for most liquid household soaps. Example: 1 teaspoon Shaklee's Basic H per gallon of water, or 1 tablespoon Ivory liquid per gallon of water.
2. Use soft water or rainwater only.

3. Isopropyl (rubbing) alcohol added to insecticidal soap increases the soap's efficiency. The alcohol penetrates the insect's waxy protective covering. Use $1/2$ cup alcohol per quart of water to dilute the insecticidal soap.
4. Spray in the evening to prevent the leaves from burning.
5. Use a high-pressure spray, not a mist.
6. Cover the plants thoroughly, top to bottom and under leaves.
7. Repeat when necessary.

STOP! DON'T THROW THAT AWAY!

The best, and possibly only, use for sunflower seed hulls

Grind up sunflower hulls and drop them into the cracks of driveways or sidewalks to prevent weeds from germinating.

Corny lawns

To prevent weed grasses, sprinkle cornmeal (preferably stale) over your plot of ground. The cornmeal inhibits germination of weed grasses, and its 10 percent nitrogen content fertilizes the soil at the same time. (Cornmeal herbicide based on research by Nick Christians, professor of horticulture at Iowa State University)

Corn-fed cutworms

Sprinkle dry cornmeal over your garden to get rid of cutworms. The cutworms eat the cornmeal but can't metabolize it, and it kills them.

Down the tubes

Use toilet paper tubes as cutworm collars to prevent cutworms from chewing plants off at ground level. Put a tube 1 inch aboveground and 1 inch belowground around young transplants.

Crawling on eggshells

Slugs are repelled by crushed eggshells spread thickly around plants.

Not what it's quacked up to be

When quack grass (an annual weed grass) is killed, it gives off a poison that kills slugs. When you pull up quack grass, throw the grass blades into your strawberry bed and leave the roots out in the sun to die. (Based on research by Roger Hagin, of the Plant Protection Research Center, Ithaca, New York)

Epsom salted slugs

Epsom salts (magnesium sulfate heptahydrate) are very bitter; they repel slugs and snails. Dissolve 3 tablespoons Epsom salts in 1 quart boiling water. Let cool, then add 3 more quarts water. Pour the solution on slug-infested areas; spray the solution on slug-infested plants. The Epsom salts will not harm the plants. In fact, Epsom salts are very good for tomatoes.

Ashes, ashes, they all fall down

Ashes repel deer, rabbits, snails, slugs, and bean beetles. Ashes also prevent scab on beets and keep aphids off peas and lettuce.

Mix wood ashes with water to make a paste and spread the paste on tree trunks to keep borers out.

Gnat and mosquito trap

Put 1 cup vinegar, 1 cup sugar, and 1 banana peel in a clean gallon milk jug. Fill the jug with water and shake well. Hang the uncapped jug in a tree.

Wormless apples

Put 1 banana peel, 1 cup sugar, and 1 cup vinegar in a clean gallon milk jug. Add enough water to almost fill the jug, shake well, and hang the uncapped jug in your apple tree before the blossoms open. The apple codling moth is attracted, but bees aren't. Replace as needed.

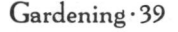

HERE LIES the body of
our ANNA
Done to Death by a Banana
It wasn't the fruit that
laid her low
But the skin of the thing
that made her go

Wormless apples, part 2

Put 1 cup vinegar, $^1/_3$ cup molasses, $^1/_8$ teaspoon sweet pickle juice or ammonia, and 1 quart water in a plastic gallon jug.

Hang two uncapped jugs in each apple tree before the blossoms open.

Finish fungus

Horseradish leaf tea kills fungus on fruit trees. Pour 4 parts boiling water over 1 part horseradish leaves. Let the tea cool, then pour it into a sprayer and use.

It's a real rhubarb

Rhubarb leaves are highly poisonous. After you have made strawberry-rhubarb pie with your rhubarb stems, boil 1 pound of rhubarb leaves in 1 quart water for 30 minutes, strain, then add a dash of liquid soap to make it stick. Spray it on aphids and spider mites to kill them.

Use rhubarb spray only on ornamental plants.

Clobber clubroot

A rhubarb stalk buried in the cabbage bed will prevent clubroot.

Tea from the tomato

Tomato leaf tea kills aphids and corn earworms, and attracts tiny, beneficial *Trichogramma* wasps. Leave 2 cups chopped tomato leaves in 2 cups water overnight. Strain the tea the next day and add 2 cups water.

Spray plants thoroughly.

NATION

Tobacco top killer, AMA study shows

By Bob Geiger
News-Tribune Washington Bureau

WASHINGTON — Tobacco is the nation's No. 1 killer and its use led to an estimated 400,000 deaths in 1990, according to a review in this week's Journal of the American Medical Association.

The study, released Tuesday, found that tobacco use causes more deaths than alcohol, firearms, motor vehicles and illegal drugs combined. Tobacco use led to roughly 30 percent of all cancer deaths, 21 percent of heart disease deaths, and 19 percent of all deaths, the study estimated.

The conclusions are those of Dr. J. Michael McGinnis, director of the federal Office of Disease Prevention and Health Promotion, and

Dr. William H. Foege. health policy fellow at the Carter Presidential Center in Atlanta and a former director of the Centers for Disease Control. They based their study on a review of medical literature from 1977 to 1993.

Diet and lack of physical activity contributed to an estimated 300,000 deaths in 1990, the study said. Alcohol led to about deaths; infectious diseases by microbial agents other AIDS, 90,000 deaths; toxic tants and contaminants, 60 firearms, 35,000; sexual behavior, 30,000; motor vehicles, 25,000; and illegal drugs, 20,000.

These factors accounted for the deaths of about half of the 2.1 million Americans who died in 1990,

the study said.

Other factors such as and lack of access to care are also important ir impact was more to measure, the doct . The study didn't estim aths due to ge-

es cause other than toxic pollu its, 60,000; behavio es.

rs pointed out that all e leading causes of lied in the study — to and lack of exercise, — result from behaves.

While the United States is expected to spend $900 billion on health care this year, studies show that less than 5 percent of that will be for prevention, the doctors said.

HAVE A CIGARETTE?

Butt out, bugs!

Cigarette butts can be soaked in water to make an extremely toxic bug spray. Nicotine is a very powerful poison that can kill just about any living creature. (In 1990, according to the American Medical Association, tobacco was the cause of an estimated 400,000 deaths and was the nation's leading killer.)

WARNING: Do not spray on crops just before harvest. *Never* use nicotine spray anywhere near tomatoes, peppers, eggplants, or potatoes; they may become infected with tobacco mosaic virus.

EXTERIOR HOUSEKEEPING

Vacuum up garden pests

Vacuum bugs out of your crops. Predator insects stay out of the way; plant eaters are slow and stay on the tops of the plants. It is preferable to use a shop vac for this so you don't get electrocuted if you vacuum up water.

There is a huge commercial vacuum, called Bug Vac, which is used very successfully in strawberry fields. There is even a Gopher Vac, which is used to vacuum gophers out of fields. The gophers are physically unharmed by this (though perhaps psychologically damaged), and are released far away from the original field.

Vacuum weeds

Dandelion seed heads can be vacuumed up to prevent dandelions from spreading. This technique works on thistle seeds too, though bear in mind that many small songbirds need thistle seeds to eat.

Use a shop vac, and plug it into a grounded plug. Often there is water outside, and you don't want to electrocute yourself.

A bright, white, dandelion-free lawn

Spreading garden lime over the lawn in early spring will prevent dandelion seeds from germinating (they need acidity). Cover the lawn lightly with lime until it is white, to change its pH. Spread the lime the day before rain is predicted. If the forecast is accurate, the lime will be washed into the soil.

Insecticidal glue spray

Mix 4 fluid ounces (one half an average-sized bottle of glue) white glue (like Elmer's) in 1 gallon warm water. Spray the glue mixture on the twigs and leaves of infested fruit trees; soft-bodied bugs, like aphids, red spider mites, scale, and mealybugs, will all

be killed. When the glue is dry, it will flake off with the dead in-sects. Repeat treatment in seven to ten days as necessary.

Which way did he go?

An aluminum-foil mulch under aphid-prone plants confuses moths, aphids, and thrips, and prevents them from landing. Light reflecting off the foil looks like the sky to the pests, and they can't tell which way is up.

MAMMAL REPELLENTS

Produce-theft deterrent

Plant yellow, orange, pink, white, or purple tomatoes, anything but red. Any human low enough to steal other people's tomatoes probably isn't smart enough to realize that a tomato that isn't red could be ripe.

Fishy

Fish emulsion, diluted and sprayed on plants, will repel rabbits (and probably attract cats).

Deer, not dear

Deer are really difficult to deal with, and we have brought much of the problem upon ourselves by replacing many old forests with young, delicious new-growth forests, and exterminating deer predators over most of the United States. The consequent cervid population explosion has turned deer into the nouveau urban pest: highly mobile; ubiquitous; almost intelligent; and often infested with nasty parasites, like deer ticks, which carry Lyme disease, and brain worms, which kill moose.

Even though a herd of up to ten deer lives in our neighborhood, our garden has never sustained any deer damage. Our two dogs would love to round up those deer and bring them home, but the deer don't enjoy being herded and stay clear of our garden.

Not all dogs are suitable for deer deterrence; it takes one with a strong sense of duty to really do the job. Even an ancient dog who could no longer run was able to prevent deer from eating the crops on his organic farm; he faithfully patrolled the perimeters of his property every day. Benji recently passed on, and his people have not yet been adopted by another dog. Their farm is now being regularly attacked by deer.

IF YOUR FAITHFUL DOG IS interested only in sitting at your feet, looking soulfully into your eyes, while deer taste your tulips and decimate your daffodils or, even worse, you don't have a dog, you may want to build a fence. Contact your local Department of Natural Resources for plans for electric or nonelectric fences that have been proven to work in your area. It is preferable to erect a fence before you plant anything tasty, so the deer never learn to dine on your property. Fences must be erected quickly, and electric ones must be juiced up immediately, or the deer will learn how to negotiate any fence under 12 feet tall.

WHILE I WAS IN the midst of writing this section on deer, I was blessed with a visitation from the Deer Goddess. Her name is Julie, and she gardens at the edge of a woods near a lake. She has a Great Dane, but he is interested only in her, not in her garden, and is useless as a deer deterrent. Over the years, the Deer Goddess and her herd of eighteen highly motivated deer-repellent testers have tested dozens of methods for discouraging deer, and during her visit she graced me with some of her knowledge:

WISDOM FROM THE DEER GODDESS

In the spring, when they are really hungry, deer will eat just about anything. In the fall, when deer are well fed and bored, they will pull out plants just for fun, then spit them out.

The Deer Goddess (artist's rendering).

Planting extra deer food away from the garden won't keep deer from eating your garden. The extra food will attract more to your area, and they will move from place to place and eat everything anyway.

Talk to your neighbors, to discover whether anyone in the vicinity is feeding the deer. If the deer are being fed, you have a political problem on your hands.

Ask what time of day the deer are appearing. Try to decipher whether they are just passing through or are a local herd. If they're just passing through, they will be less persistent than a local herd would be.

The Horror!

Some scare tactics, like whirligigs, recordings of barking dogs, or fluttering reflective ribbons, will work on deer that are just passing through. Local deer will eventually learn to ignore these things.

Deer are not repelled by offal from their butchered brethren, nor by antlers with part of the skull still attached, even if the skull is still bloody.

Repulsive

Blood meal repels deer, but attracts dogs. The dogs may do more damage than the deer.

Marking your territory

Filthy human hair will repel deer. Clean hair doesn't smell bad enough.

Strong, fresh human urine doesn't deter deer. Fresh timber wolf droppings don't work either unless the wolves are actually living on the property.

Rough it up

A stick fence that is only 5 or 6 feet high will keep deer out if the ground on the other side is very uneven. A steep slope, a rock garden, mounds, or holes on the inside of a hard-to-see-through fence will all prevent deer from risking the jump. A deer with a broken leg is a dead deer.

The Deer Goddess grows hops on her fence. The strong, oily smell of hops repels deer.

Gotcha!

Mousetraps hung from tasty trees at deer-browse height will deter the deer. The traps need to be checked and reset regularly.

The Deer Goddess's mousetraps are tastefully spray-painted blue and embellished with gold stars. They did duty as Great Dane–repelling Christmas tree ornaments before being transferred outside.

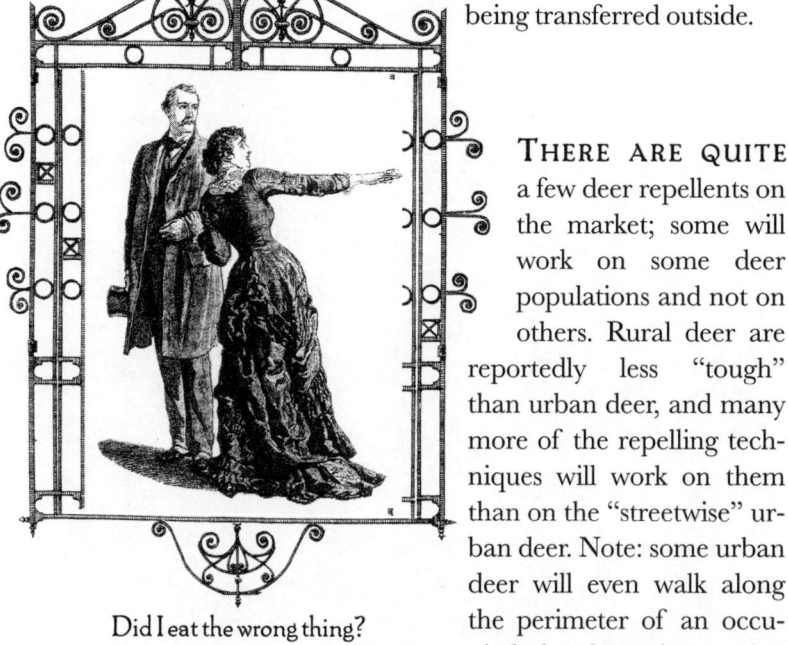

Did I eat the wrong thing?

THERE ARE QUITE a few deer repellents on the market; some will work on some deer populations and not on others. Rural deer are reportedly less "tough" than urban deer, and many more of the repelling techniques will work on them than on the "streetwise" urban deer. Note: some urban deer will even walk along the perimeter of an occupied dog kennel, taunting the dogs. If the dogs were loose, the deer wouldn't even dare to set hoof on the property.

At a store near you

The most highly recommended commercial product is Tree Guard, which is a bittering agent in a very durable latex base. It reportedly only has to be applied twice a year, and has been extensively tested and found to be nontoxic to soil bacteria.

Well-soaped limbs

In a study of deer repellents, conducted at the Smithsonian's National Zoological Conservation and Research Center in Front Royal, Virginia, in 1987 and 1988, one of the most effective repellents was Lifebuoy bar soap.

Leave the soap in its wrapper, drill a hole in it, put a wire through the hole, and hang the soap in a tree. If you have a very severe deer problem, you may want to hang several bars in your trees. Space the bars about $2^1/2$ to 3 feet apart.

Smells too good

Aromatic oily herbs (rosemary, scented geraniums, lavender, etc.) planted around tasty plants repel deer. The deer can't afford to get the aromatic oils on themselves, as the strong odor would prevent them from smelling danger.

Smells too bad

For a homemade deer repellent, dissolve 2 teaspoons beef bouillon and 2 well-beaten eggs in 1 gallon water. Let the mixture sit and rot for a couple of days. When it gets really stinky, it's ready to use. Spray it on your fruit trees; respray after heavy rain.

This mixture would probably repel other mammals besides deer: like me, for instance.

Deer exclusion

Surround your rose garden or orchard with wire fencing rolled out on the ground. You can even lay it over a few stumps or logs; just don't let the fence lie flat; allow it to billow up. The deer's hooves can get caught in the holes in the fencing, and they will be very reluctant to try to cross the barrier.

Fishing for deer

Pound some stakes into the ground and string up clear, heavy-duty fishing line every 3 or 4 feet about three feet above the ground. The deer can't see the line, it catches their legs, and scares them.

Fall fashions for conifers

Deer can wreak havoc on evergreen seedlings and saplings in the winter when snow cover makes grazing difficult. You can protect your saplings by making them wear little paper caps. I can hear them complaining now: "Aw Ma! Nobody else has to wear a hat! It'll embarrass me in front of my friends." In the spring, when their friends have been mowed down by deer, you can say, "I told you so."

Each fall, fit the young conifers with natty paper caps: fold a quarter-sheet of typing paper around the terminal bud of the tree so the top of the paper is $1/2$ inch above the top bud. Staple the paper tightly in place with at least three staples; each staple

should hold some needles. The paper will hold together all winter, then disintegrate in the spring rains. In Germany the saplings' little winter caps are made of raw wool twisted over the buds; woollen caps will not disintegrate during wet weather.

Once your saplings' terminal buds are above the deer-browse level, they can forgo their protective headgear.

In the winter, the Deer Goddess lays wormwood (*Artemisia absinthium*), an exceedingly bitter member of the daisy family, over young cedars and white pine to protect them from deer. Deer won't touch trees that are covered with wormwood.

Be careful when handling wormwood; many people are severely allergic to it.

RACCOONS

Three sisters

Corn that is interplanted with melons, squash, or cucumbers gains some protection from raccoons. Stickery squash leaves are unpleasant for the raccoons' tender little paws, and the raccoons can't see over the big-leaved plants. Grow beans up the cornstalks; the nitrogen from the beans' root nodules will help fertilize the corn, and the bean stems will help anchor the corn.

Native Americans, who first developed corn, squash, and beans, grew these crops in symbiotic relationship in the same garden plot, the beans growing up the corn, the squash planted between the rows.

Hair of the dog

Save Fido's hair to use in the garden as a raccoon repellent.

EWW!

Don't wash that stinky, sticky, stiff undershirt! Not yet anyway. Hang it in your garden to repel raccoons. Replace it with a stinkier one frequently.

TOO STINKY FOR A GROUNDHOG

Evict groundhogs (alias woodchucks) from under your buildings by placing a bowl of cleaning ammonia in the area they are using. The fumes will drive them away almost immediately, and they won't return.

After your groundhogs have been evicted, you can keep them out of your vegetable garden with a 6- to 12-inch-tall fence; groundhogs are very fat and short-legged. They are also very fond of clover; if you plant some outside your garden, it will distract them from your beets.

TOO STINKY FOR GOPHERS

Gophers are also repelled by ammonia. Place ammonia-soaked sponges in their entrance holes.

TOO STINKY FOR SKUNKS

Skunks eat armyworms, tobacco worms, white grubs, cutworms, potato beetles, grasshoppers, mice, snakes, crayfish, slugs, and snails. But . . . !

Place a bowl of cleaning ammonia in the crawl space to drive skunks out from under your buildings. Interestingly, these smelly creatures cannot stand strong smells.

SKUNKED DOG

Wash the victim with laundry soap, rinse with vinegar and water, rub baking soda into the dog's fur, then rinse. (Our dog got skunked last summer. The baking-soda chaser really helped.)

CASTOR BEAN WARNING: Castor beans are often promoted as an effective mole and gopher repellent. I do not recommend planting castor beans. All parts of the castor bean plant are poisonous, particularly the seeds. Two or three seeds can kill a child, six seeds can kill an adult.

Once during a short plane trip I sat down next to a woman I had not seen for a couple of years. She immediately said, "You were right about castor beans! Last time I talked to you, you tried to discourage me from planting them, but I planted them anyway, because they're so pretty. They almost killed my dog!"

She explained that she hadn't thought castor beans would be a problem because her dog had never bothered any of her plants. But one morning she discovered that all her castor bean seedlings had been pulled up during the night, and her dog was lying almost dead in the yard. She brought the dog to the vet, where it was diagnosed with castor bean poisoning. She still isn't sure whether the dog pulled up the seedlings, or whether it tried to eat the critter that ate the seedlings.

BIRD REPELLENT

Cornell University researchers sprayed ripening blueberries with sugar water. The sugar-sweetened fruit sustained 50 percent less bird damage than unsugared fruit did.

Fruit-eating birds can only digest simple sugars like fructose; sucrose gives them a stomachache.

The recipe: dissolve *11 pounds* sugar in 1 gallon warm water, let it sit until the solution looks clear and the sugar has completely dissolved. Then spray the solution onto ripening blueberries, strawberries, or other fruit. (I couldn't believe that 11 pounds of sugar could really dissolve in a gallon of water, but I tried it out in my kitchen, and it can!)

PET REPELLENTS

Shoo, Fifi!
A rotten potato makes a good dog repellent, and will probably repel bad dogs as well.

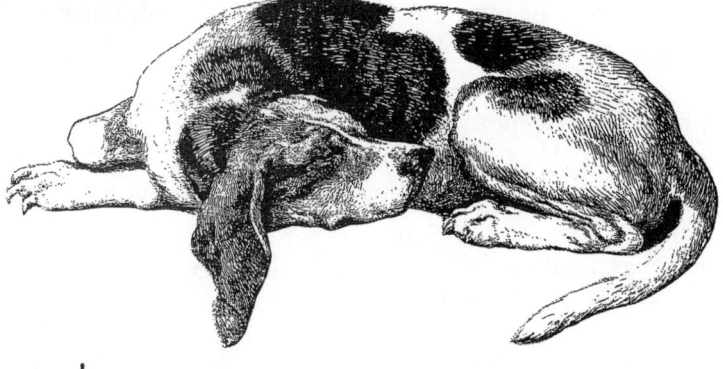

Scat, cat!
Keep Felix out of your houseplants by putting a lemon oil–soaked cotton ball at the base of the plant.

I said SCAT!
Scatter ground-up grapefruit or lemon rinds on the soil of your newly planted garden to repel cats.

PET TRAPPING

Come back, little Sheba!
If your pet mouse, gerbil, or hamster gets loose in the house, smear the inside of a big stainless steel bowl generously with butter. Put bait in the bottom of bowl. Make a ramp up to the rim of the bowl with books or a board.

HELPFUL
GARDEN DENIZENS

Every good bug does fine

Beneficial insects need moisture. Put pans of water in the garden, and change the water daily. Spray plants with a 10 percent

sugar solution to attract predatory insects. The predators will think the sugar is aphid honeydew, and will eat all your aphids.

Ladybugs on patrol

Ladybugs and their larvae are the best natural controls of aphids. Ladybugs can be bought by mail order, but it is sometimes difficult to convince them to stay where you want them.

To encourage ladybugs and other insect predators, plant tall flowers and flowering herbs like dill and cilantro in a border around your garden—the predatory insects like to hide in these plants.

If it slows down, step on it

An old English gardener, being interviewed by the BBC about identifying bugs in the garden, said: "If it moves slowly enough, step on it; if it doesn't, leave it—it'll probably eat something else."

Splendid grass

John A. Pickett and colleagues at the Institute of Arable Crops Research in Rothamsted, England, and the International Centre of Insect Physiology and Ecology in Nairobi, found that molasses grass (*Melinis minutiflora*), planted in sorghum and maize fields, both repels stem-borer pests and attracts parasitic wasps, which lay their eggs in the stem borers. Only 5 percent of the intercropped maize plants were damaged, compared with 39 percent in a maize monoculture.

Stinging wasps

The insects most people are fearful about are the large wasps such as hornets, yellow jackets, and other paper wasps. The smaller wasps, like the *Trichogramma* wasps and the ichneumons, are purely beneficial to humans.

The hornets, yellow jackets, and other paper wasps are also beneficial, since the insects they feed their larvae are mostly harmful species. But try telling someone who has just been stung that the wasp is mostly beneficial!

These wasps are beneficial as long as they stay away from us and our loved ones. The wasps that invade our space usually must be eliminated.

Wasp traps

In early summer, wasps are looking for protein to feed their young (meat, dog food, etc.); later in summer, they are looking for sugar for themselves. If sweet traps are attracting bees, switch to meat.

Sting prevention

Don't leave sweets or soda pop around. Compost food scraps, and cover them well with dirt or finished compost. Pick up and compost overripe fruit. Don't feed pets outside.

Yellow jackets can be pests at picnics. Females are very short-tempered and will sting at the slightest provocation. Don't let the provocation be that you swallowed one with your soft drink! When eating outside, drink through a straw, not directly out of a can or bottle of soda pop.

Flight control

Hang sticky flypaper in the wasps' flyways. When the traps are full, and preferably at night, remove the flypaper by putting a paper bag over it, then putting the paper bag in a plastic garbage bag. Seal the garbage bag tightly and let it bake in the sun the next day.

Funneled wasps

Put a funnel into a jar, or cut off the top of a plastic soda bottle and invert it on the open top of the bottle. Put a piece of meat or some soda into the bottom of the jar or bottle, and lube the inside of the funnel with WD-40 oil.

Bowled over

If you can find the opening to the wasps' nest, cover the opening at night with a clear bowl set firmly into the ground. The workers will be confused by their inability to escape, and will not dig a new hole. The nest will starve.

Just desserts

A naturalist working for the East Bay Regional Park System in Oakland, California, poured honey near the entrance holes to underground yellow-jacket nests in one of the regional parks at dusk. Next morning all the nests had been dug out and the wasps and brood eaten by skunks or raccoons. Skunks and raccoons relish bee brood.

Feed the cannibals, tuppence a bag

Beneficial nematodes thrive in healthy, humus-rich soil. Highly organic soil has more nematode enemies, like cannibal nematodes and fungi that lasso harmful nematodes with sticky protein loops. The more organic material you have, the more good nematodes you'll have to eat the bad nematodes.

His mama told him not to pick up hitchhikers

Don't kill any caterpillars that have little white cocoons stuck to their skin (like tiny grains of rice). The cocoons house tiny parasitic braconid wasps, which are digesting the caterpillar.

Help, Anty Em!

If your house is being attacked by termites, YOU NEED ANTS! Ants and termites are mortal enemies; ants will patrol the perimeter of a house to keep the termites from establishing colonies. There is really no reason to kill ordinary ants outside; fire ants and carpenter ants do not count as ordinary ants.

Ants eat the eggs and larvae of fleas and flies, caterpillars, and conenose bugs (conenose bugs are also known as Big Bedbugs and Mexican Bedbugs; conenose bug bites can cause severe allergic reactions in some people, and can also transmit parasites that cause a debilitating disease called Chagas' disease).

For thousands of years, Chinese citrus growers have been bringing ants into their orchards to prey on caterpillars and other pests. They even provide the ants with bamboo runways from tree to tree.

The more I learn about ants, the more I like them. I think I will go outside and put out some wholesome ant food right now!

Eight legs, eight eyes (or six or four eyes) and all heart

Spiders are incredibly useful creatures. Among other things, they eat flies, bedbugs, moths, grasshoppers, and cockroaches. Every day, spiders eat a combined volume of insects that outweighs the combined weights of all people on earth. Each autumn, Chinese farmers, who obviously know who their friends are, build little straw teepees in their fields to house hibernating spiders.

There are three thousand species of spider in the U.S. Only two of the species are dangerous to humans: the black widow and the brown recluse. Avoid spider bites by shaking out shoes and clothing before you get dressed.

Spiders prefer a tranquil, undisturbed existence, and are shy and unaggressive. If you leave them alone, they will leave you alone. Luckily for all of us, they will not leave the insects alone.

Leggy pest control

Centipedes eat slugs, snails, and other pests. In the tropics, 1-foot-long centipedes also eat mice, birds, and geckos.

A short while ago I asked my friend Liz, who is a commercial greenhouse manager, to find me some slugs for testing purposes. After a protracted search of the greenhouses, she found two slugs and two snails. There were three or four adult centipedes, plus some babies, under each board in the greenhouses instead of the usual mob of slugs. She had recently stopped killing the centipedes.

Glow-in-the-dark pest control

If your garden is being lit up at night by luminous caterpillars, you may be witnessing the parasitic nematode *Heterorhabditis* at work. A bioluminescent bacteria that lives in the nematode's gut causes massive infection in the caterpillar, making it glow at night.

More glowing

Firefly larvae, which are often luminous, feed on insect larvae, slugs, and snails.

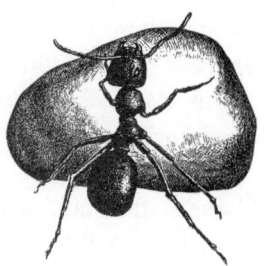

Decorative pest control

In the summer of 1996, entomologists Anurag A. Agrawal and Richard Karban glued tufts of cotton on the undersides of the leaves of cotton plants. The artificially

What if the baby isn't all right?

tufted plants produced 30 percent more cotton than the untufted plants did.

Eggs and nymphs of predatory insects were found in the glued-on cotton, and there were five times as many predatory adult bugs on the "decorated" plants than on the undecorated plants. There were fewer spider mites and more cotton bolls on the decorated plants.

Agrawal and Karban suggest that since some wild cotton species sprout their own underleaf tufts, it may be possible to breed or genetically engineer the trait into cultivated cotton.

I am not growing cotton, and I don't want to wait for tomatoes to be genetically engineered, so this summer I am going to decorate my vegetable garden with pom-poms and see what happens!

Hide and seek

Plant the largest variety of plants that you can. Helpful predatory insects like a variety of plants to hide in.

A flowery carpet

Flowering groundcovers planted around fruit trees will attract the tiny wasps that are predators of moth larvae and eggs.

HELPERS WITH BACKBONE

Toadying to toads

Toads are extremely helpful predators that eat slugs, snails, insects, and even mice. Each toad can eat ten to fifteen thousand bugs per season. Toads absorb water through their skin; so a small pond or a shallow pan of water will encourage them, as will brushy places to hide. A light near a footpath increases a toad's nocturnal hunting success.

Toad Hall

Make a toad house by knocking a chunk off the top of a medium-sized clay flowerpot and turning the flowerpot upside down. The hole formed by the missing chunk is the toad's door.

Reptiles are our friends

Snakes and lizards will be happy to eat insects, gastropods, and small mammals in your garden, and will benefit from the water and underbrush you have provided for your toads.

Unclenching an annoyed snake's jaws

Our neighbor's sister loved snakes as a little girl. The child once carried a garden snake around for two and a half hours before the exasperated reptile finally chomped down on her hand and refused to let go. The girl's parents couldn't pry the snake's jaws open. Neighbors told them to dip its tail in boiling water. When they did, the snake let go and disappeared.

WARM-BLOODED HELPERS

Fine Feathered Friends

Chew the fat, eat the borers

Hanging suet in your trees is like putting out a WELCOME WOODPECKERS! sign. The woodpeckers will come to eat suet and stay to eat borers.

Grasshopper ambush

Put a 10 percent molasses solution in a container (1 part molasses to 9 parts water). Grasshoppers will be attracted to the sweet water. Set out bread crumbs or birdseed near the dish of molasses water. Birds will come for the seed and stay for the 'hoppers.

FINE FURRY FRIENDS

Batter's up!

Bats are the most important predators of night-flying insects. Since many of the insects that prey on gardens and gardeners are night flyers, bats are some of the gardener's best allies in the war on pests. Each bat can eat between a quarter and half of its weight in insects every night; a single Little Brown bat can eat more than five hundred mosquitoes in an hour! If you are lucky enough to have even a small colony of twenty or so bats on your property, over twenty thousand mosquitoes, or a smaller number of heavier insects like beetles, gnats, moths, or flies, could be consumed by bats in your vicinity every warm summer night.

Thou shalt covet thy neighbor's bats

Seduce your neighbor's bats by making a bat house. Request bat-house plans from your local Department of Wildlife, or

Department of Natural Resources. Or get a copy of Merlin Tuttle's book, *America's Neighborhood Bats.*

In cold, short summer climates, bats need warmth: make your bat house thin, but long and wide, and use a nontoxic dark paint or stain for maximum solar gain when you hang it in full sun, high up out of the reach of predators (at least 15 feet up a wall, for example).

In hot climates, make your bat house airier, paint it a light color, and hang it in the shade.

Maybe if there are enough bats in your garden, your apples won't have worms in them.

Shrews

Shrews look like pointy-nosed mice with lots of sharp teeth, tiny eyes, and short velvety fur, like moles'. The largest shrew in the U.S., the Short-tailed shrew, weighs from $1/2$ to 1 ounce. The Pygmy Shrew weighs $1/8$ ounce.

Shrews spend most of their lives underground, hunting insects day and night. They eat up to twice their own weight every day and can starve to death in only three hours. (Human teenagers only *think* they're going to starve to death every three hours.) The shrewy diet includes moth and beetle larvae, slugs, snails, spiders, fungus, centipedes, sow bugs, earthworms, crickets, and even mice and smaller shrews. A 1-ounce shrew is capable of eating as much per day as does an average housecat!

Make sure those mice you're trying to trap are really mice, not shrews, since shrews can actually be frightened to death by capture or a loud noise.

A little night music.

The mole patrol

Moles, like shrews, are insectivores.

Night and day, summer and winter, moles are on patrol, using their keen senses of touch and smell to find their prey: earthworms, insects, centipedes, sow bugs, Japanese beetles and their larvae, cutworms, wireworms, slugs, snails, grubs, beetles, and ants.

Many gardeners hate moles, because of the tunnels they dig. But mole tunnels help aerate the soil, so it absorbs water more efficiently, and the tunnels are generally soft and easily flattened with a lawn roller. The amazing amounts of invertebrates moles can eat per day makes them much more useful than harmful.

With Friends Like Us, Who Needs Enemies?

If six legs are better than four, then some frogs really are achieving Better Living Through Chemistry. But where does that leave the one-eyed frogs? And the two- or three-legged frogs?

Revenge of the Six-legged Frogs

In the summer of 1995, schoolchildren on a field trip to a nature preserve near Henderson, Minnesota, discovered severely deformed frogs.

Twelve-year-old Guthrie Swenson said later, "Some had two front legs but only one back leg. Some had three back legs; some had four. A few had only one eye. And one frog had a back leg that was normal in length but was webbed the whole length. It was pretty weird." This is an experience I would really like my children to forgo!

In the following month, more than two hundred deformed frogs were captured near Henderson; scientists estimated that 30 to 40 percent of the frog population were deformed.

By 1999, deformed amphibians had been reported in more than thirty states, three Canadian provinces, and Japan. Deformed frogs have been found in more than half of Minnesota's eighty-seven counties.

Seventy percent of the frogs in one Minnesota pond had deformities. This compares with a historical "background" level of less than 1 percent. Frogs that had already died of their deformities were not available for comment, and did not participate in the census.

Martin Ouellet, of McGill University in Montreal, in a seven-year-long study, examined almost 30,000 frogs along a 150-mile stretch of the St. Lawrence River valley. According to Ouellet, "It's quite obvious that there is a problem in sites subject to pesticides." He said, "It's everywhere, everywhere there's an association with pesticides."

Nearly three thousand years ago, in his Works and Days *(this translation is by David Grene), Hesiod wrote:*

Do not piss into the waters of rivers that flow to the sea nor into the springs; avoid this very carefully; neither shit into them; that would be far from well for you.

And, according to Hesiod, the greatest possible blessing was:

Their women give birth to children like their parents.

WAIT A MINUTE, YOU'RE NOT DONE 'TIL YOUR TOOLS ARE PUT AWAY

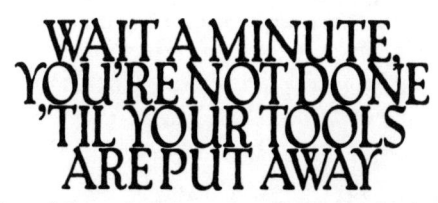

My husband and I used to lose so many gardening tools in tall grass or ground cover when we were landscaping that he spray-painted all our tool handles safety orange. Sometimes even that didn't work. I think we needed to attach helium balloons to all the handles.

PUT THEM AWAY CLEAN

Like a well-oiled machine

Fill a bucket with sand, pour in enough mineral oil to saturate the sand. After scraping the dirt and mud off your garden tools, plunge them into the oily sand to keep them clean and rust free.

Get the rust out

Vinegar will clean rust off your tools: soak the afflicted tool, bolt, etc., in white vinegar overnight. Scrub off the rust in the morning.

Sanded handles

Keep your tool handles well oiled and sanded down; if you don't, you can remove a small splinter by painting it with a thin layer of white glue. Let the glue dry, then peel it off. This works for wood and fiberglass slivers as well as for small thorns.

HOUSEKEEPING

THIS CHAPTER CONTAINS information on how to deal with specific nonhuman household pests. Methods for discouraging pesty humans are not within the scope of this book.

HOUSEHOLD PEST REDUCTION

One million species of insects have been described; scientists estimate that there are another nine million insect species yet to be discovered by humans. There may be a billion insects on earth at any given time; insects outweigh humans twelve to one.

One third of all pesticides in the United States are used in households. Homeowners may spray hundreds or thousands of

UNPLEASANT COMPANY

AND HOW TO GET RID OF IT

times the amount of pesticide per acre on their property than commercial farmers do.

A sense of pest proportions

There are vast differences in the danger posed by different pests. A wasps' nest under the porch roof is a potentially fatal threat to someone with a bee-sting allergy, but a line of black ants trundling across the bathroom floor is not an emergency. No one in the history of the world has ever died directly from black ants, though ant-killing poisons have certainly been fatal to many small children and pets.

This section is divided into three parts: Dangerous Pests, which are those that can harm human beings directly; Destructive Pests, which can cause property damage; and Nuisances, which annoy us by their presence, but do not harm humans, and cause little or no property damage.

DANGEROUS PESTS

Mosquitoes

Mosquitoes are some of the most dangerous *animals* of any kind known to man, since their bite can transmit malaria, yellow fever, encephalitis, and other diseases.

Female mosquitoes lay their eggs in standing water. One pint of stagnant water can brood five hundred wrigglers (mosquito larvae). If you pour all the water out of even the smallest containers at least twice a week, you will kill the mosquito eggs and larvae. Change pet water every day. Bring old tires to your local waste-disposal authority.

Mosquito trap

Put out a pail of soapy water—when the female lands to lay her eggs, she won't be able to get out again.

Oil on the waters

Mosquito wrigglers can't breathe if there's a thin layer of oil on the water. Use vegetable oil, please, not motor oil.

Gulp!

Goldfish or minnows in your pond or rainbarrels will eat the mosquito wrigglers.

HOUSEFLIES

Adult houseflies suck up liquids containing sweet or decaying substances. Adult females lay their eggs in moist manure or garbage. When the charming fly children hatch, they feed on the moist food around them.

Typhoid Mary's best friends

Almost all of the flies caught in houses are houseflies. Houseflies can transmit typhoid fever, cholera, dysentery, pinworms, hookworms, tapeworms, and the bacterium that causes ulcers.

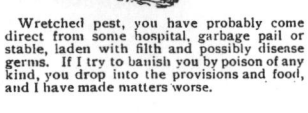

Wretched pest, you have probably come direct from some hospital, garbage pail or stable, laden with filth and possibly disease germs. If I try to banish you by poison of any kind, you drop into the provisions and food, and I have made matters worse.

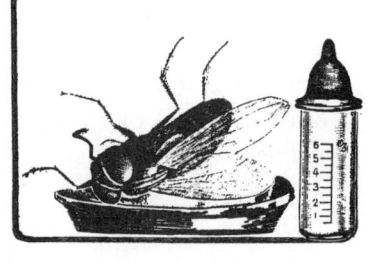

Fly exclusion

Put tight-fitting screens on doors and windows; quickly repair holes in screens.

Clean 'em out

Store food in covered containers.

Rinse out food containers before recycling them. Wash

garbage cans; keep garbage tightly lidded. Separate wet garbage from dry garbage. Store meat leftovers in the freezer until garbage day, and put them out right before the garbage is collected. This will also discourage raccoons and dogs from digging in your garbage can.

Compost your vegetable scraps, but cover them with a layer of dirt or finished compost to avoid setting up a fly nursery.

Sour flies

Keep a spray bottle of vinegar near the sink to down flying insects. If the fly is near the window, you can wash the window afterward.

Sticky flies

Hang a sticky flypaper (which comes in little cardboard tubes, and can be bought at feedstores and hardware stores) from the ceiling in the middle of the room.

Sucked-up flies

Use your vacuum to do in that annoyingly loud fly that won't stand still to be swatted.

Soused flies

Stale beer with a little sugar added can also be used as fly bait. The trap itself is made by cutting fly-sized entrance holes into a 1-quart plastic beverage bottle. Cut the holes 1 inch apart, into the black plastic part of the bottle, 1 inch below where the black plastic meets the clear plastic.

Flies fly upward toward the light after feeding, and with the small entrances in shadow, they can't find their way out. Leave the plastic label on the bottle to create more shade.

LICE

These tiny trespassers are not just disgusting; they can transmit typhus and relapsing fever.

Pickled lice

Head lice can be killed off by wrapping the afflicted head in a vinegar-soaked towel. (Do not remove the head before doing this; it should remain attached to the body, no matter how angry you are at your child for bringing lice home!) Cover the wet towel with a dry towel and leave on overnight.

The vinegar dissolves the lice and their eggs so they can be shampooed away the next day. Everyone in the household should be treated at the same time. All towels and bed linens should be washed with hot water, and all the furniture should be vacuumed.

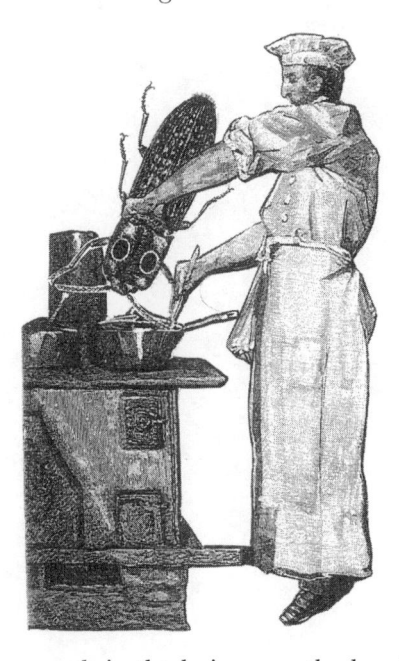

Oiled lice

Lice are killed by coconut oil. To get rid of head lice, wet hair, apply a shampoo containing coconut oil, lather thoroughly, rinse. Repeat, but leave suds in the hair, wrap the head and hair in a towel, leave on for $1/2$ hour, remove the towel and comb the hair with a nit comb. Wash the hair again and rinse.

Make a Clean Breast of It

Breast cancer rates in industrial countries have risen by 1 percent every year since the dawn of the chemical age, in 1940.

Just in case male readers happen to be feeling smug, I offer the following statistic: the National Cancer Institute reports a 126 percent rise in prostate cancer between the years 1973 and 1991. This is a 3.9 percent rise in the incidence of prostate cancer per year.

A study from the Indiana University School of Medicine published in 1997 showed that β-HCH (a variant of the active ingredient in the pes-

ticide lindane, used in lice killers) spurred the growth of breast cancer. A 1990 study in Helsinki found that breast cancer patients had more β-HCH in their fat than was present in women without cancer.

The 1999 edition of the Physicians' Desk Reference *contains this warning about lindane (capitalization theirs):*

WARNINGS: LINDANE PENETRATES HUMAN SKIN AND HAS THE POTENTIAL FOR CNS [central nervous system] TOXICITY . . . IN EXCEEDINGLY RARE CASES SEIZURES HAVE BEEN REPORTED WHEN USED ACCORDING TO DIRECTIONS . . .

Progress!

Many over-the-counter delousers now contain pyrethrins (ground up painted daisies), or permethrin, which is a synthetic pyrethrin. These products should be far safer than lindane-containing prescription lice killers.

TICKS

These arachnids can transmit Lyme disease, Rocky Mountain spotted fever, and other similar diseases from one animal to another. Since ticks can ride you and your pets into your house, a little outdoor housekeeping may be in order.

Ticked off

Guinea fowl eat ticks! They also make good watch birds, and conveniently roost in trees at night, well above marauding foxes.

I don't care that a guinea fowl's proportions aren't graceful, any enemy of ticks is a friend of mine.

Tickicidal bedding

Deer mice host juvenile Lyme disease–transmitting deer ticks.

Soak cotton with a pet shampoo or lotion containing permethrin, and put the treated cotton in a cardboard or plastic tube in a sheltered spot where the deer mice are likely to find it. The mice use the cotton to line their nests, and the permethrin kills the ticks.

FLEAS

These minuscule athletes can carry many diseases, like the bubonic plague and typhoid fever .... NEVER CRUSH FLEAS WITH YOUR FINGERNAILS.

Cleanliness is next to flealessness

Flea larvae feed on dried fecal blood of the parent fleas, as well as on dirt and debris. If there is nothing to eat, the flea larvae will not mature.

Vacuum up those fleas. Put salt or pyrethrum or boric acid in the vacuum-cleaner bag to kill off the fleas. Seal up the vacuum bag, and put it in the sun.

Salted fleas

Pour noniodized salt into the cracks in your floor to kill fleas. Wall-to-wall carpeting can be salted with 6 pounds salt per 100 square feet; leave the salt on for twenty-four hours, then scrub the rug with strong soap.

Having children is a very serious business.

Salty rinse

When washing rugs and the cover to your dog's bed, add salt to the rinse water. If your pet sleeps in the same place every night, wash the cushion cover in hot water every day.

Let us fly, said the flea

Sand fleas are repelled by lavender oil. To drive fleas and sand fleas from a house in the summer, sprinkle oil of lavender on rugs and floors and turn up the heat.

Bathtime for Fido

A good long BATH will drown many fleas

(sorry, Fido). Soap or Safer's Insecticidal Soap or pyrethrum or shampoos containing D-limonene (citrus oil) will all kill fleas.

Lemon aid

Three recipes for homemade D-limonene flea and tick killer:

1. Cut up 2 lemons and pour boiling water over them. Let the lemons soak overnight. Sponge the lemony liquid over your pet—it kills fleas on the Spot.
2. Score the skin of an orange and rub the citrus oil right onto your pet.
3. Liquefy 3 or 4 orange or lemon skins in the blender with 3 cups boiling water. Let the mixture cool before sponging it onto your pet.

You may want to wear protective gloves when you sponge homemade D-limonene onto your canine or feline, to protect yourself from your pet. Dogs and cats hate the smell of citrus.

THE THREE PESTKETEERS: ROACHES, RATS, AND ANTS

These three types of pests all are attracted by similar conditions. Don't tempt them.

If your dwelling looks like you are waiting for a visit from the health department, you are providing a prime cockroach, ant, and rodent habitat. Remove stacks of newspapers; stored magazines; piles of old clothes, cardboard boxes, and used grocery bags. (Pretend your in-laws are coming for a visit.)

Don't leave food out overnight, keep surfaces clean, keep food in the refrigerator or freezer or in tightly sealed containers, keep appliances clean, wash dishes promptly, sweep or vacuum frequently. Wash pet bowls after their meals.

Fix faucet drips and bolt toilet bowls securely to the floor to prevent leaks. Wrap pipes to prevent condensation. Put strainers over sink, shower, and bath drains (roaches and rats can both live in sewers). Seal up utility and pipe entrance holes with caulk.

Habitat prevention

Don't stack firewood or lumber near the house. Thin out ground-covering vegetation near the house, especially ivy. Keep garbage cans tightly lidded, and take out garbage every night. Compost your food scraps, burying them under several inches of dirt or compost.

COCKROACHES

These rather large insects can contaminate food just by crawling over it. You don't really know whose toilet that cockroach visited last. Cockroaches are also suspected of causing allergic reactions in some people, and may be one of the reasons so many inner-city children have asthma.

Dusted cockroaches

Sprinkle boric acid or borax in cockroach runways, out of the reach of pets and children. Spread the boric acid thinly and evenly over a wide area so the roaches won't detour around it. Roaches will avoid large clumps of boric acid.

Blow boric acid into cracks and crevices, using a plastic ketchup or mustard bottle as a high-tech application device. Apply very lightly, as if salting your meal. Wear a mask and goggles when applying dust. The borax works indefinitely.

Roaches are not repelled by boric acid and have not developed resistance to it after decades of use. Roaches, unlike some of the people who have them, are very clean; as they preen themselves, they will ingest any boric acid that is sticking to them. The boric acid poisons them. It also scratches and damages their exoskeletons, so they desiccate.

Borax is a formulation of boric acid that can be bought in grocery stores. *Boric acid* can be found in drugstores. Boric acid won't harm people or pets unless they ingest a lot of it.

Mopping up

Mop floors with borax and water. Sponge down walls with the solution.

Roach bait

Mix 1 cup borax, $\frac{1}{2}$ cup flour, $\frac{1}{4}$ cup powdered sugar, and $\frac{1}{2}$ cup cornmeal. Keep the bait away from children and pets. A couple of likely spots for bowls of roach bait are under the refrigerator and behind the stove.

Petrified pests

A mixture of $\frac{1}{2}$ cornstarch and $\frac{1}{2}$ plaster of Paris kills roaches.

Trap dancing

At bedtime, dampen a rag or cloth with beer and place the rag on the floor in an out-of-the-way place. Cockroaches will congregate under the cloth. Dance *La Cucaracha* on the cloth in the morning.

REST
IN
PIECES

Exploding cockroaches

Mix $\frac{1}{2}$ cup baking soda with 1 tablespoon powdered sugar. Put the mixture in roach areas, out of the reach of children and pets. Roaches eat the mixture and explode! This works on silverfish too.

RESEARCHERS IN CALIFORNIA DISCOVERED that in restaurants with regular pesticide spraying programs, cockroaches were five to ten times more tolerant of organophosphates and up to three hundred times more tolerant of carbamates than normal. Unfortunately, the human beings who work in the restaurants are still quite sensitive to these poisons.

Organophosphates are modified nerve gases, which were discovered by accident as by-products of nerve gas research in Germany in the 1930s. Organophosphates are responsible for 80 percent of the pesticide-related hospitalizations in the U.S. every year.

Carbamates are a broad class of chemicals used as insecticides, fungicides, or herbicides. They are less acutely toxic than organophosphates, but they have been shown to break down into highly carcinogenic compounds.

Why even consider using anything as dangerous as a carbamate to kill cockroaches, when you can do something as fun as:

Rube Goldbergian Roach Control

Skewered!

Pour some beer in a bowl. Carefully balance long wooden skewers or broom straws around the edge of the bowl. The roaches will climb up the sticks. When their weight tips the skewers, the roaches will fall into the beer and drown.

Depressed roaches

Put bait on an inverted container in the middle of the bowl. Half fill the bowl with soapy water. Make a hinged teeter-totter ramp out of a tongue depressor by taping the underside of the tongue depressor to the outside of the bowl. Calibrate the teeter-totter so it is very, very slightly heavier toward the outside of the bowl. (You could balance it perfectly across the top of the bowl, then put a small piece of tape on the outer end of the tongue depressor.)

After the roach teeters into the bowl, the hinge resets the ramp for the next victim.

YOU DIRTY RAT!

The Old World rodents that were accidentally introduced into the New World—the black rat, the Norway rat, and the house mouse, are among the major scourges of mankind. They act as transportation systems for lice and fleas, which harbor diseases.

Those Who Knew Him Best Deplored Him Most

Petrified mice and rats

Mix 1 part plaster of Paris and 1 part flour with a little sugar and cocoa powder. The rodents eat the snack, drink a little water, and then get plastered! Place in an area inaccessible to children and pets.

After I first published *Slug Bread,* I received a call from a man who wanted to stump me. He asked whether a scavenger that ate a plastered dead rat would die itself. The answer is probably no, because the chemical reaction of the plaster of Paris would be over, and it would have become a hard lump of plaster that would retain its shape.

DESTRUCTIVE PESTS

Webworms and Tent Caterpillars

These moth larvae are known as armyworms where I live, because in bad years, they really invade. Pull down webby masses of worms in the spring and STOMP! before the caterpillars defoliate every plant in sight.

Termites

These wood eaters thrive on damp and rotting wood. Improve your drainage, keep your foundation dry. Keep all wood painted. Don't let any wood come in contact with the soil. Store firewood and lumber away from the house. Stack firewood on a poured concrete foundation. Crawl spaces under the house need adequate ventilation to keep them dry. Repair all cracks in the foundation.

Sand barrier

Subterranean termites find it impossible to tunnel through sand; it makes their tunnels collapse. Pour several inches of 10- to 16-mesh sand all around your foundation. The sand barrier has been widely tested in Hawaii, and has been included in Honolulu's building code.

Deadly rivalry

Don't forget that the termite's greatest enemy is the ant. If you have termites, put out your WELCOME ANTS mat.

Nuisances

The following pests are simply pesty. Relax, no one is going to get sick or die because of them.

Ants

Invasion prevention

Clean the kitchen, wash the dishes, rinse off sticky-sweet jars and bottles, put away leftovers, and wipe the counters with vinegar.

Pull up the drawbridge

If the ants are already in your house, put your pot of honey and pet-food dishes in bowls of water to make anti-ant moats. A little dish soap in the moat water helps.

A veritable taste explosion

Equal parts of dry baking soda and powdered sugar will kill ants.

Ant killer

Mix 1 cup water, $1/3$ cup sugar and $1 1/2$ teaspoons boric acid, and shake well. Fill small bottles with cotton balls and saturate the cotton with the poison. Poke small holes in half the lid so ants can get in. Place the bottles on their sides in ant-infested areas. The ants will bring the bait back to the nest to share, thus killing off the colony.

Place the bottles where they will be accessible to ants but

inaccessible to children and pets. Under the refrigerator would be a good spot, as would under the kitchen sink, if your under-sink cabinet has a childproof latch.

This mixture will also kill carpenter ants, which do not eat wood, as termites do, they merely build their houses in it.

Ant-ade

Blend citrus peels with water, strain, and put in a spray bot-tle, or put a little citrus solvent in a spray bottle of water. These citrus sprays will kill the ants.

Boiled ants

A single queen, lurking deep in her nest, perpetuates the whole colony. Your mission is to kill her and so eradicate the nest. You are not allowed to use any chemicals to complete your task. What do you do?

Answer: Very quickly, in order to avoid swarming workers, shovel off the top layer of the anthill. Immediately pour boiling water into the nest. Run! Any surviving worker ants will die of old age in a week or so. If the colony is still alive in a week, try again.

Ant farms

Are your ants farming aphids or scale insects? Hose off the aphids or use a soap spray on them. Paint tree trunks with a band of grease, lard, petroleum jelly, or Tanglefoot (Tanglefoot is extremely sticky stuff that is sold in garden centers, hardware stores, and through mail order. It is used to make sticky traps.) Tanglefoot can be removed from hands with cooking oil.

Anti-ant spray

Brew concentrated mint tea and use it instead of water to di-lute Safer's Insecticidal Soap to the proper amount. Put the mixture in a spray bottle. It kills ants on contact, and repels their survivors.

Diversionary tactics

A small open bottle of honey at the base of the infested plant will make ants lose interest in aphids. Keep the bottle full.

Shallow pans of water left outside may encourage thirsty ants to stay out of your house.

Meat, no potatoes

Red imported fire ants are meat eaters. Mix boric acid in with bacon grease or other meat grease, and put it in small glass jars with ant-sized holes in the lid. Put the baited jars in areas where you have observed the fire ants.

Silverfish

Cleanliness is next to silverfishlessness

Silverfish like damp basements. Their menu includes ant and termite larvae, flour, wallpaper paste, glue, linen, silk, rayon, and dirty clothes. Light, cleanliness, and good ventilation repel them; unfortunately, this means you will have to clean out your basement, vacuum your books, and blow boric acid into any cracks you haven't already treated for ants.

The good news is that silverfish like to eat starched clothes. What a perfect excuse not to starch clothes!

His previous job as a pesticide applicator came back to haunt him.

Silverfish trap

Smear some Tanglefoot on a piece of cardboard, and place a small pile of oatmeal in the middle. Rub cooking oil on your hands to remove the Tanglefoot.

Clothes Moths

Clothes moth larvae need stains on clothing—food, sweat, hair, oil, urine, starch—to get enough vitamins and minerals to develop properly. They are attracted by dirty clothes; store clean woolens only.

Vacuum corners, cracks, crevices, heating and air ducts, closets, and storage areas. Clothes moths are often attracted to carcasses of dead animals. Poisoning rats and mice may lead to a clothes-moth infestation. Try trapping the rodents instead.

Moth repellents

Moths are repelled by cedar and dried lavender.

Like a moth to light

Make a simple trap: after dark put a flashlight in a bucket, turn the flashlight on, and aim it upward. Find a clear glass bowl that will sit securely in the top of the bucket above the lit flashlight. Fill the bowl with slightly dish-soapy water. Leave the flashlight on all night. The moths will dive into the beautifully lighted swimming pool but, being unable to swim, will drown.

Fishing for moths

Clothes moths are attracted to fish oil. Unwind flypaper onto a piece of cardboard and place little bits of fish or sardine oil on it.

Shake, rattle, 'n' roll

Webbing clothes moths can destroy piano felts. Playing the piano every day dislodges the eggs.

Well-seasoned moths

Salt rugs heavily, then vacuum. Salt helps destroy moths. Or wipe rugs with a cloth dampened in a strong salt solution.

Freeze 'em

If you live in a very cold climate, your heating system may be keeping moths alive in the winter. When the outside temperature is less than 0 degrees F, take moth-infested furniture and clothing outside and leave it there or in an unheated garage for a week. The pests will freeze to death.

Flour and grain weevils

Check food for bugs before putting it away. Store food in tightly sealed containers.

Spice up your life

The U.S. Department of Agriculture's Stored Products Research Laboratory in Savannah, Georgia, has done studies indicating that coriander, dill, cinnamon sticks, lemon peel, and black pepper repel or kill some insects in stored grains. The plants probably evolved their lovely spiciness as insecticides and insect repellents.

Shaken pest syndrome

Insects do not like to be disturbed. Stir grain and flour, turn the bags upside down, thump them. "Did you remember to thump the grain today, dear?"

Fruit Flies

Fruit fly eggs are present on most fruit, especially on bananas. Never leave fruit peels, especially banana peels, out. Refrigerate or dispose of overripe fruit; seal it in airtight containers before you compost or bury it.

If you do get a fruit fly infestation, the vacuum cleaner is your best friend. Fruit flies are so soft-bodied that they don't survive vacuuming.

Trapped

Sticky flytraps work well for fruit flies. So does setting out a jar of half vinegar, half grape jelly with a pinch of baker's yeast sprinkled over it.

The morning after a party many people discover that sweet wine in the bottom of an open bottle can also be used to trap fruit flies.

CREATIVE HOME ECONOMICS

I hated "Home Ick" in junior high school. This chapter is my revenge for the "Mother-Daughter" fashion show and the fake cinnamon rolls. They should have let me take wood shop!

Every year, $8.8 billion is spent in the United States on toxic cleaning products whose manufacture spews thousands of tons of toxic waste into the air and water. The average American uses more than forty pounds of these toxic products per year.

According to the U.S. Office of Technology Assessment, 15 percent of all toxic pollution in the wastewater stream comes from private homes.

MORE BAD NEWS

According to the National Center for Health Statistics, there has been an increase in respiratory cancers and respiratory diseases in homemakers over the past forty years. The increase was attributed to the use of toxic cleaning products, since homemakers tend to be less likely to smoke than the general population.

MORE!

Most poisonings that occur in the home are caused by cleaning products, and most of the victims are under the age of six.

THE GOOD NEWS

Your common kitchen ingredients and household appliances have uses that June Cleaver never dreamed of. All the equipment and ingredients you need for a clean, nontoxic house are probably already in your home; they were in your grandmother's home too.

A clean home is not something "to die for"!

1 OZ. PREVENTION > 3 LB. CURE

According to Don Aslett, a professional cleaner and author, there is a 50-to-1 ratio for cleanup time compared to prevention time. I am all in favor of cleaning prevention rather than cleaning; I have much more fun things to do with my time than try to clean ketchup stains out of a white blouse. (Not wearing white blouses is a definite probability here.)

After doing exhaustive research, I am amazed at what a strong correlation there is among stain prevention, accident prevention, and good manners.

No-food zone

Declare part of your house off-limits to food. Your bedroom wastebaskets will not breed fruit flies because banana peels have been thrown in them, you will not find disgusting cups of mold on windowsills, or rotten tangerines buried under piles of dirty laundry. Chocolate bars will not melt onto your child's radiator. Soft drinks will not spill on the bed.

You will be depriving your children of the true joys of living in squalor until they go off to college, but that's what college is for, isn't it? To broaden our horizons?

Trash prevention

If you use paper towels, buy the unbleached kind and compost the used ones. Bleached paper towels may cause a build-up of dioxins in your compost pile.

Use cloth napkins, they're more absorbent and will avert some wiping-on-sleeves activity.

Use real plates, not paper plates: washing dishes takes less time than cleaning up after collapsed paper plates.

Off with their shoes!

Get good doormats. Use them. Train your family to remove their shoes just inside the door. This will keep your house much cleaner.

Emergency room avoidance

Pot handles should always be turned toward the back of the stove.

Cooks should not wear loose long sleeves or billowy clothes that could catch on pot handles or brush over the hot stove and catch fire.

Bloodstain prevention

Don't set up your own accidents. For instance, don't leave a hammer on top of the ladder, then move the ladder. Head wounds bleed a lot and bloodstains are hard to clean off the carpets and clothing.

Wear work clothes, then you won't have to worry so much

about perspiration stains, or grass stains (or whatever other kinds of stains your work causes).

Ketchup stain prevention

Before pouring ketchup, insert a drinking straw all the way to the bottom of the ketchup bottle, then remove the straw. The air tunnel will allow the ketchup to flow freely out of the bottle.

Egg stain prevention

Spin an egg to see if it's hard-boiled. Hard-boiled eggs spin quickly; raw eggs barely spin. Labeling eggs after you hard-boil them also helps.

Mural prevention

Get washable markers, crayons, paints. Better yet, do not let your young children color unsupervised. Put the art materials out of their reach. Do art projects with them. Your walls, furniture, and light-colored pets will thank you.

LAUNDRY AND MISCELLANEOUS TEXTILE CLEANING

Mauve boxer short prevention

Sort laundry into whites, darks, light colors, etc.

I do the patriotic-laundry sort: red, white, and blue. Do not let wet laundry sit and mildew in a pile or in a hamper. Mildew stains.

Lint and stain prevention

Empty all pockets before washing clothes. Tissues make very unattractive lint, which sticks all over your clothes; and watches, pens, Kleenex, and gum do not wash well.

Draw the line here

Draw over ring-around-the-collar with white chalk before throwing the shirt in the hamper. The chalk will absorb the grease before the shirt is washed.

Remodeling prevention, or, how many towels can fit into a linen closet?

Answer: many more than you think. Roll up your towels and sheets instead of folding them. Rolled towels take up half as much space as folded ones do. Now all our linens actually fit into our linen closet, which was a laundry chute in its previous incarnation.

CLEANUP

Okay, you failed. Your children use their shirtfronts as napkins, you forgot to hide the felt-tipped pens when you were done with them, the puppy's housetraining isn't coming along as well as you would like it to.

Really gross stains

You know what they are: Rover isn't housebroken yet; Junior's dinner disagreed with him; Susie got punched in the nose; Fluffy got into the garbage; Fifi met a skunk, then rolled on the carpet. All these organic messes provide food for bacteria and fungi.

Buy a combination bacterial/enzyme product that is designed to eat these organic pet and human messes. Pet supply stores and janitorial supply stores carry these products, usually designated as "pet mess" cleaners. The product must be a combination of bacteria and enzymes. Clean up the bulk of the disaster, then mix up a batch of live bacteria and enzymes, which will eat the stain left from the deposit. Follow the directions on the label exactly.

Gummy couches

Remove gum from upholstery by chilling the gum with ice cubes, then scraping off the hardened gum.

If your child is young enough to wear a diaper, don't give her gum!

Scribbled-on sofas

Remove ballpoint pen ink from upholstery or carpeting by covering the stain with salt and vacuuming the salt up as the stain is absorbed. Repeat the process until the stain is gone.

ALTERNATIVE USES FOR KITCHEN INGREDIENTS

BICARBONATE OF SODA, ALIAS BAKING SODA

Destinked sinks

Deodorize sinks by pouring baking soda and boiling water down the drain.

Freshened carpets

Deodorize a carpet by sprinkling baking soda over it and vacuuming the soda up one hour later.

Cleanser replacer

Use baking soda sprinkled on a damp sponge for kitchen or bathroom scouring chores.

Sparkling silver

Fill an *aluminum pan* with a mixture of 1 teaspoon baking soda and 1 teaspoon salt per cup of hot water. Submerge your silver in the hot solution for a few minutes, rinse, and wipe with a soft, dry cloth. The aluminum acts as a magnet to attract the tarnish away from the silver. Very tarnished silver may have to be done several times. Strips of aluminum foil in a glass or steel pot filled with the hot solution will also work. If you have large silver pieces to clean, cover the bottom of your stoppered sink with a sheet of aluminum foil, and fill the sink with hot water. Pour in the salt and baking soda mixture, then let your candlesticks have a relaxing soak.

Burned pots and pans?

Sprinkle baking soda liberally onto burned pans, then moisten with water. Wait several hours and the burned crust will lift right out.

Clean a coffee pot

Fill the pot with cold water, add 1 teaspoon baking soda, boil for a couple of minutes, then pour out the water and rinse the pot out well with clean water.

COFFEE?

Smoke

To remove smoke smells from a couch, sprinkle coffee grounds on the upholstery, wrap the entire couch in plastic, and seal it so it is airtight. Let it sit overnight or longer, then vacuum up the coffee grounds and shampoo the couch.

And what are you doing smoking on the couch anyway? It's dangerous.

Open containers of coffee grounds will also deodorize your car.

Frozen coffee

Deodorize your freezer by leaving an open cup of coffee grounds in the freezer overnight. Remove the coffee grounds and repeat the next day if necessary.

CONDIMENTS AND CABBAGE

Hold the mayo in your sappy hands

Mayonnaise will remove pine pitch, tree sap, grease, or tar from your hands or your car: rub mayonnaise on the sticky skin or car finish, let it sit a few minutes, then wipe it off.

Tasty furniture

Mayonnaise will also remove crayon marks from wooden furniture: rub mayonnaise on the marks, let sit for a minute or two, then wipe it off with a damp cloth.

Smooth as butter

Remove oil paint from your hands by rubbing them with butter! Don't ruin a whole stick of butter for this purpose; cut off a small piece to use for paint removal. This would be the ideal use for rancid butter, but butter never lasts long enough at our house to go rancid.

Hurry and ketchup!

Use ketchup to polish copper or brass. Pour some ketchup on a rag, then polish the copper or brass with it. Worcestershire sauce works for this too.

Cabbage polish

Polish your pewter by rubbing it with cabbage leaves.

VINEGAR

Don't wash windows while the sun shines

It makes streaks. Wash windows using 10 parts white vinegar to 1 part water sprayed from a bottle. Wipe the windows dry using crumpled newspaper to keep the windows from streaking.

The father's nightmare.

Wipe out mildew

Spray mildew with vinegar water solution. Then wipe it right off.

Foodborne microbes

Foodborne microbes trigger 81 million cases of disease per year in the United States, according to the General Accounting Office (GAO), an investigative arm of Congress.

When tested, fresh bean sprouts averaged more than ten million coliform bacteria per gram of sprouts. Average counts of sixteen million *Listeria* and *Aeromonas* bacteria per gram of radish were also found.

Susan S. Sumner, of Virginia Polytechnic Institute in Blacksburg, West Virginia, found that washing tainted produce in water "is better than doing nothing—but not a whole lot better." Even washing the sprouts three times did not drop the coliform counts enough.

Sumner contaminated apples with a strain of deadly *E. coli* bacteria known as O157:H7. She was then able to eliminate all of the bacteria by dipping the fruit in a nontoxic mix of vinegar and off-the-shelf hydrogen peroxide. The O157:H7 strain of *E. coli* has been implicated in the deaths of people who consumed contaminated apple cider or hamburgers.

Other researchers have demonstrated that a drenching spray of vinegar, along with a drenching spray of hydrogen peroxide, will effectively kill bacteria on produce. It makes no difference whether the vinegar or the peroxide is sprayed first.

Vinegar and hydrogen peroxide will also kill *Salmonella* bacteria, so use those spray bottles to clean your sink and cutting boards after you prepare your chicken.

LOW-TECH WINS AGAIN!

Microbiologists Dean Cliver and Nese Ak, of the University of Wisconsin at Madison, tested cutting boards to see whether plastic or wooden ones were more hygienic. They doused plastic and wooden cutting boards with raw chicken juice spiked with live bacteria broth, and discovered that the bacteria thrived for hours on the plastic cutting boards, even after the boards were washed in hot, soapy water. The same bacteria died out within three minutes on wooden cutting boards, even if the wooden boards were not washed! (Keep washing your cutting boards, plastic or not!)

Cliver and Ak are investigating the possibility that wood fibers dehydrate the bacteria and kill them.

Sour ants

Repel ants by wiping counters down every day with cider vinegar. If your castle has marble counters, instruct your maid not to wash the counters with vinegar. Vinegar dissolves marble.

Cleaning compound

Pour $1/4$ cup baking soda, $1/2$ cup white vinegar, and 1 cup clear ammonia into 1 gallon hot water. It's good for cleaning floors, woodwork, and greasy stoves; kills mildew; and doesn't need to be rinsed off.

Squeaky clean

Clean tubs, sinks, and toilet bowls with full-strength white vinegar.

Volcano in a sink

To clear a clogged drain, pour $1/2$ cup baking soda down the drain, then 1 cup white vinegar. The vinegar and baking soda will react chemically, releasing carbon dioxide, which causes the vinegar to fizz. After the fizzing stops, pour a kettleful of boiling water down the drain.

The squeaky dish has no grease

Vinegar added to dishwater prevents grease from clinging to dishes.

Oven grease repellent

Prevent grease buildup on oven walls by wiping the walls with vinegar on a damp cloth.

Withdraw the deposits

Clean out mineral deposits in copper teakettles: boil 1 part vinegar and 1 part water in the kettle, let soak until cool, then pour out and rinse with clean water.

Laundry softener

Add 1 cup white vinegar during the rinse cycle.

Prevent diaper rash

Soak diapers in vinegar and water in the diaper pail, and then add 1 cup vinegar to the wash water. The vinegar helps kill off the bacteria that cause diaper rash.

Clean pet urine out of carpets

Combine 3 tablespoons white vinegar, 1 quart warm water, and a drop of dish soap. Apply the solution gently to the vicinity of the "accident" with a rag. Blot dry with thick rags.

NEVER MIX VINEGAR OR AMMONIA WITH CHLORINE BLEACH OR WITH CLEANSERS CONTAINING CHLORINE! POTENTIALLY FATAL CHLORINE FUMES CAN BE EMITTED. In fact, chlorine bleach and cleansers containing chlorine should never be mixed with anything other than water.

Some dishwashing liquids contain ammonia, which reacts with chlorine. Check the labels before using dish detergents with other cleansers.

CONTROLLING NONHUMAN INDOOR PESTS

(Read Dr. Spock for How to Control Children)

SOAPS, TOILETRIES, LAUNDRY AIDS, AND DETERGENTS

The soaps, shampoos, and other toiletries that we use affect the quality of the water that goes down drains and, eventually, into our waterways. They can also affect our own health more immediately, since some of what we put on our skin is absorbed into our systems.

The breakdown products of the chemicals in some beauty products and laundry and dish detergents can form nonylphenols, which are hormone disrupters. Dish soap, laundry soap, and washing soda are all much safer than detergents.

Many shampoos and other "beauty products" can also contain formaldehyde. Formaldehyde may improve the beauty of embalmed corpses and dissected frogs, but I don't think it could really improve the looks of live human beings! Read the labels of "beauty products" before you buy them. My motto is: unless there's a pressing medical reason, I don't put anything on my skin or that of my children that isn't safe to eat.

Luckily, there are many brands of dish soap, laundry soap, shampoos, hand lotions, and other "beauty products" that contain safe ingredients; they can easily be found in health food stores and co-ops. Just read the labels.

Here are some novel uses for "beauty products."

A beehive hairdo
Knock down and kill wasps and bees by spraying them with hairspray.

Avon's Skin-So-Soft

Using this bath oil as a mosquito repellent is a well-known folk remedy in Minnesota, land of ten thousand lakes and trillions of mosquitoes. Apparently, the fragrance molecules in Skin-So-Soft are exactly the right size to clog up mosquito antennae so the mosquito's sense of smell stops working.

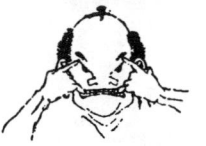

DEET

DEET is a pesticide used as a mosquito repellent. The British medical journal *Lancet* published research that pointed out that slurred speech, staggering gait, agitation, tremors, convulsions, and death have all been documented consequences of DEET use. (Thanks anyway, I'll just scratch!)

Grease repellent for auto mechanics

Rub 1 or 2 tablespoons liquid dish soap over your hands and arms before working on a car. Let the soap dry before you start to work. When you're ready to clean up, use more dish soap, and the grease will wash right off.

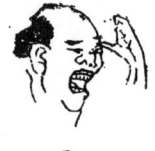

MORE GOOD NEWS

A study of eleven different pollutants, conducted by reproductive endocrinologist Benjamin J. Danzo, of the Vanderbilt University School of Medicine in Nashville, Tennessee, found that some environmental contaminants can bind to both estrogen and androgen receptors, as well as to binding proteins for other hormones.

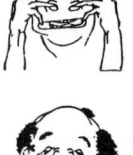

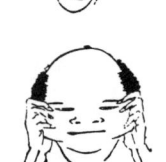

Danzo stated that the possibility that some pollutants can affect more than one hormone

receptor at a time means that exposures much smaller than those previously believed to be harmful may combine to cause damage.

Toxicologist Devra Lee Davis, of World Resources Institute in Washington, D.C., stated that if these hormone mimics were to have an effect on humans, "it would most likely occur in rapidly dividing cells," such as in the fetus, young children, or sperm-producing tissue. "It may even have an influence on the sex of children or the ability of couples to have children."

HURRY UP WITH THAT CLONING RESEARCH, WILL YOU?

In 1997, Shanna H. Swan, of the California Department of Health Services in Emeryville, reported that all her team's analyses of male fertility data show a decline in sperm counts since 1970 for men in Western countries.

The new declines average more than 1 percent annually, or about 1.5 million sperm fewer per milliliter of U.S. semen, and 3 million sperm fewer per milliliter of European sperm.

NOT MANY OF US LEFT, AND WE'RE NOT TOO BRIGHT, EITHER

Diane S. Henshel, an Indiana University neurobiologist, found huge differences in the left-to-right-brain symmetry of heron chicks hatched from eggs collected near a dioxin-spewing pulp and paper mill.

Laboratory-grown chicks exposed to dioxins also develop lop-sided brains. Henshel's group has linked these asymmetries to behavioral changes in chicks, even in chicks with low dioxin exposures.

Michael Gilbertson, of the International Joint Commission in Windsor, Ontario, said that he has found gross deformities in dioxin-exposed birds, such as twisted beaks, missing eyes, and clubbed feet. But, he says, "what's interesting here are the structural deformities in the brain," because there have been reports of cognitive problems in dioxin-exposed children.

And finally, something no household should be without:

CITRUS SOLVENT
(Grandma would have loved this stuff)

Citrus solvent is a relatively new product on the market, marketed by different companies under different names. It is the concentrated oils from citrus peelings, and seems to be able to degrease just about everything from stoves to car engines. It can be used full strength for really tough jobs (check first that it won't stain or dissolve the object you are trying to clean), or diluted for more delicate jobs, like cleaning walls or floors. I tried it out on the bubble gum on a neighbor's chin, and the gum came right off, leaving the chin as good as new. It is also great for removing the adhesives that stay on new bathroom fixtures for years after the labels are removed.

I think citrus solvent also shows great promise as an environmentally sound herbicide and pesticide: I tried it on slugs, and they died quite quickly; but when I tested the citrus solvent out on a houseplant to see whether it could be used to kill pests on plants, it melted my plant.

HOUSEPLANTS ARE OUR FRIENDS

A 1989 EPA report stated that "sufficient evidence exists to conclude that indoor air pollution represents a major portion of the public's exposure to air pollution and may pose a serious acute and chronic health risk." Since some people spend 90 percent of their time indoors, indoor air pollution may be a more serious health risk for many people than is outdoor air pollution. Many materials found in modern homes, such as synthetic carpeting and carpet backing, plywood, paneling, and pressed board, release formaldehyde and other volatile organic chemicals into the air.

Dr. Bill Wolverton, senior research scientist at the National Space Technology Laboratories in Mississippi, found that common foliage plants can remove contaminants from the air in houses. The plants deliver airborne toxins to the microbes living around their roots. These microbes then break down the toxins.

Recent research also shows that plant-filled rooms contained 50 to 60 percent fewer airborne molds and bacteria than rooms without plants.

Wolverton estimates that fifteen to twenty plants would purify the air in the average energy-efficient house.

Don't overfertilize

Too much nitrogen encourages plant suckers like mealybugs, aphids, whitefly, scale, etc.

Scat, scales!

Brush buttermilk or sour milk on the infested area with a cloth or paintbrush. Wait an hour, then rub the scale off into a container. Seal the container and throw it away.

Alcohol kills

Mealybugs on houseplants die if you touch each bug with an alcohol-soaked cotton swab.

So do cigarettes

Plastic-bag an infested plant, and have a smoker blow cigarette smoke into the bag. Quickly seal up the bag, and all the mealybugs, spider mites, aphids, and whiteflies on the plant will croak. Point this phenomenon out to the smoker.

Peel out

Cucumber peelings will get rid of black ants. Spread the peels around ant trails in your house; the ants eat the peels and die.

CREATIVE USES FOR HOUSEHOLD EQUIPMENT

Organic pesticides are made of natural materials and biodegrade rapidly so they don't accumulate in the environment. However, they are still poisons, or they wouldn't kill "pests." The safest way to get rid of pests is to do it the old-fashioned way: squash 'em.

As modern twenty-first-century citizens, we have acquired sophisticated household equipment that can be used to do things the old-fashioned way. No, I am not talking about breadmaking machines; I refer to even more common equipment, like central heating, vacuum cleaners, and glue.

When my son was a brilliant nine-year-old, he came up with a novel pest control idea at a barbecue: he skewered a grasshopper, roasted it, and ate it. He roasted one for me and it wasn't bad, but I think some hot spices would have improved it.

Don't be too disgusted at the idea of insectivory. Worldwide, it is much more common for people to eat insects than not to eat them. However, if you are going to barbecue a delicious insect, make sure that your neighbors haven't been using pesticides. Many insect pests are resistant to pesticides; an insect may be flying around quite happily with a dose of pesticides in its body that could make you sick.

THE VACUUM CLEANER

Sucked up

Houseflies, fruit flies, and mosquitoes can be removed from your home by vacuuming them up.

Yellow jackets could also be vacuumed up with a shop vac, but put several inches of hot soapy water in the bottom of the vacuum canister first, to make sure that the insects don't emerge alive! Plug up the vacuum hose after vacuuming until you are sure there are no survivors.

Flying dandruff

Whiteflies can be vacuumed off your houseplants or out of your garden or greenhouse.

Wrap the end of a vacuum nozzle with bright yellow electrical tape. Turn on the vacuum, and shake the plant while holding the nozzle above the plant. The whiteflies are attracted to the yellow nozzle, and will be sucked up.

THE FURNACE
Hot air treatment for household insects

A temperature of 120 to 130 degrees F will kill most insects. On a very hot sunny day, evacuate all humans, pets, and houseplants from your home; close all your windows and doors; open all the drapes; and remove all flammable materials from near your furnace. Then turn the heat on high for six hours.

Don't let anyone else back in the house until the heat is turned off, the windows are open, and the house has cooled down.

BARBECUE
Charcoal lighter fluid is nasty stuff

One piece of household equipment that every red-blooded, nontoxic, barbecuing family should own is a chimney starter for getting charcoal briquettes going.

A chimney starter is a metal cylinder with a handle; crumpled newspaper is put in the bottom of the cylinder, and the briquettes go on top of the paper. You light the paper, and in half an hour the briquettes are ready to pour into the barbecue. It's a much cleaner, safer, and cheaper way to start the coals than using charcoal lighter.

Many hardware stores carry these chimney starters, and they can also be mail-ordered.

Must busters

Banish musty odors from closed-up cottages, closets, and fridges by leaving out an open pan of charcoal briquettes. The briquettes can still be used for barbecuing after they have been used to soak up odors.

More Good Reasons to Avoid Chemicals

AUTOIMMUNE DISORDERS

Autoimmune disorders, such as rheumatoid arthritis, can be induced in laboratory animals by exposing them to very small doses of chemicals that are considered nontoxic by themselves. In combination, these chemicals can over-stimulate the immune system into an allergic overreaction in which the body attacks its own connective tissues. The body responds to real and imagined enemies in what has been called "cellular paranoia." The more chemicals that are loose in our environment, the more likely we are to get sick.

Are your cells paranoid?

VARYING TOXICITY

"It can sometimes take a thousand or ten thousand times as high a dose to produce toxicity in one animal as in another. This difference is very important to consider when we are thinking about using toxicity data from animal experiments and applying them to human beings."
—Dr. Michael A. Kamrin, Toxicology: A Primer

THALIDOMIDE

Thalidomide, the infamous sedative that caused horrible birth defects in the 1950s and early 1960s, was originally believed to be safe because in laboratory tests, pregnant rats and mice treated with the drug produced normal offspring.

One of my grade school classmates was a "lucky" thalidomide child: he was only missing parts of fingers instead of entire limbs.

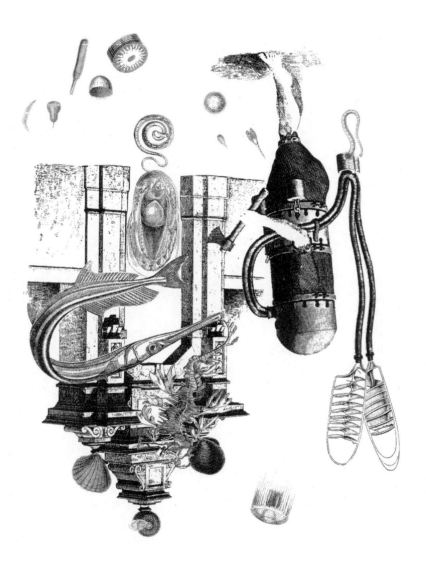

GORY AND DISGUSTING

I HAVE SAVED THE BEST for last (yes, I eat my cake first, and then the frosting). This chapter is my favorite. Please do not assume from this that I am a bloodthirsty monster. Those who object to the ideas contained within this chapter would do well to contemplate the alternatives. Is it really better to have a quick, "clean" kill due to poison, which can continue to kill and maim other creatures long after the target organism is dead? (Imagine a dopey poisoned rat being caught and eaten by your cat.) Or is it better to be more intimate with the creatures you're dealing with, to get your hands dirty, but leave your environment clean?

You will notice that this section contains some methods for killing some of the creatures that have already been described as beneficial. I am not advocating killing these creatures, I am merely acknowledging that some people will want to rid their property of them.

It is indeed better to use nonchemical pest control rather than synthetic poisons, but think hard before you meddle on a large scale. Even the organic insecticides like rotenone, pyrethrum, nicotine, sabadilla, and *Bacillus thuringiensis* (Bt), should only be used cautiously and in the evening. The organic pesticides break down safely, but can have unintended victims before they decompose. Just about everything except Bt is toxic to honeybees, and Bt is toxic to all caterpillars, not just pest species.

Even handpicking pests can have its drawbacks: I once squashed dozens of ugly-looking spiky caterpillars which were defoliating my Dusty Miller plants. Later, when we looked up the caterpillars in a guide book, I discovered, to my horror, that I had massacred dozens of baby painted lady butterflies! I bet E. B. White had lots of painted lady butterflies on his farm in Maine, where he described himself in *One Man's Meat* as: ". . . a man who hardly dares shoot a crow for fear of upsetting the fine adjustment in the world of birds and insects, predator and prey."

According to Chaos theory, which is revolutionizing science, it is possible that a butterfly waving its wings could affect the weather halfway around the world a month later. Even archie the cockroach understood this when he quoted the spider:

> *"curses on these here swatters/what kills off all the flies/me and my poor daughters/unless we eats we dies"*

My daughter strongly objects to my tests of various pest-killing techniques. She informs me that I'm mean. I don't particularly enjoy the testing either. Following a single ant as it wanders in our garden, so I can see whether the concoction I've sprayed on it is killing it, induces mixed emotions. I want the recipe to work, but on the other hand, ants, when closely observed, are endearing little creatures. And the suffering of sprayed slugs is simply pathetic.

On Borneo, spraying insecticide to eradicate malaria killed off more than mosquitoes. The Dyak people's villages were left catless almost overnight when their cats, whose principal food was cockroaches, ate poisoned roaches. Rodents quickly became so numerous and fierce that they began to attack children.

If you really want to be scared out of your wits, try reading the labels on garden pesticides and herbicides. It's illegal to use the stuff without reading the labels, but almost no one who uses it ever does read them . . .

Think of the following as pest control Charles Addams would have approved of.

WE HAVE OUR METHODS...

Kids! Don't swallow that gum!

Wrigley's Juicy Fruit gum is fatally attractive to moles.

While wearing gloves to prevent human scent from getting on the gum, unwrap the gum and roll it into a cylinder. With a stick, poke holes 4 to 6 inches apart in the mole's run, and drop a gum cylinder into each hole. The moles love Juicy Fruit gum, no other flavor will do, but it clogs up their intestines and they die. (Originally published in the newsletter of the Dawes Arboretum in Cincinnati, Ohio)

The exsanguination of Mr. Mole

Thorny sticks pushed into mole burrows can kill the inhabitants. Mole blood does not coagulate well, and they bleed to death if cut.

Is it time to pay the piper?

Before you kill your moles, remember that they are insectivorous and probably eating a lot of harmful insects in your soil. Try to learn to live with them. You can use a lawn roller to flatten their tunnels in the lawn, and they really aren't noticeable anywhere else.

Pickled slugs

Fill spray bottles with a half-and-half solution of vinegar and water. Go into the garden at night with flashlights and spray the slugs with a "stream" setting. The vinegar causes the slugs to slime to death. If your children are slightly sadistic they may enjoy slug hunting.

The Night Patrol
searching for pests.

Slug bread

Pour 3½ cups lukewarm water into a large bowl, and add 1 package (1 tablespoon) baking yeast. Let the yeast dissolve, then add ¼ cup sugar, 2 teaspoons salt, and 4 cups flour. Mix well, and let it sit for a while as you find some empty plastic milk jugs with lids. Cut a few quarter-sized holes about halfway up their sides. Pour an inch of the slug bread into the jugs. Then go out and bury the jugs in your garden so the holes are sitting just above ground level.

The slugs are attracted to the smell of the fermenting dough, crawl in the convenient holes in the sides of the jug, and never get out alive! Pour out the slug bread when it gets really disgusting, and pour in some fresh dough.

Shocked slugs

Slugs will not cross a barrier strip of flexible copper 3 inches high buried 1 inch deep in the soil. The moist, slimy slugs get an electrical shock whenever they touch the copper!

Sloshed slugs

Pour a couple of inches of stale beer into the milk-jug slug trap described above. The slugs will drown happy.

Squashing boards

Two boards on top of each other, but separated by a couple of stones, make a deadfall trap for slugs and snails that hide under the top board. In the morning, remove the stones and stomp on the boards. Leave the dead gastropods to attract more. Slugs and snails are attracted to dead kin.

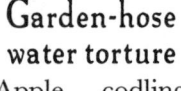

Squash bugs

Squash bugs and harlequin bugs are true bugs (shield shaped). Bait squashing boards (see above) with cucumber peels for squash bugs, and with cabbage leaves for harlequin bugs.

Garden-hose water torture

Apple codling moth larvae and aphids can be killed by directing a strong spray of water directly at the trunks of afflicted trees. Pay special attention to rough and loose bark.

Lovely, lovely fish heads

Gophers are repelled by fishheads placed in their burrow (and who wouldn't be?). (From *Gardening Without Poisons,* by Beatrice Trum Hunter)

Eat 'em up, yum!

Decaying meat or fish inside a clear plastic beverage bottle makes a good housefly trap. Put an inch of soapy water in the bottom of the bottle.

Bursting beetles

Dust plants with dry wheat bran or cornmeal early in the morning to control Colorado potato beetles. The beetles eat the bran, drink, and then burst when the bran expands.

Fermented insects

Handpick offending insects, crush them, and let them rot in a jar of water under the afflicted plants to repel others of their kind. (From *The Bug Book*, by Helen and John Philbrick)

Beheaded thistles

If you cut the head off a thistle just as it starts to bloom, it will bleed to death.

THE BLENDER
Bug juice

Capture a cup or two of your least favorite insect. Use only one species per batch; do not mix and match! If you can find insects that don't look healthy, pick them especially; their ground-up carcasses may infect other insects with viruses. Always wear rubber gloves when dealing with bug juice. A cloth or paper mask may not be a bad idea either. You are dealing with germ warfare here.

Off with their heads!

Place insects in a (retired) blender with 2 cups lukewarm water and liquefy. Strain the goo through cheesecloth or a fine sieve that is not used for food; dilute $1/4$ cup bug juice with 1 or 2 cups water.

Spray afflicted plant on both sides of leaves, along stems and runners. Repeat treatment after rain. Spray bug juice in the evening only, as sunlight may kill the insect viruses.

Clearly labeled leftover bug juice may be frozen to use later.

Do not use the bug juice blender for food ever again! (From *Rodale's Garden Problem Solver*)

Though children often enjoy the gory and disgusting stuff the most, actually this whole book is for children. Children, with their rapid growth rates and high rates of cell division, their immature immune systems, and their high respiration and metabolic rates, are more susceptible to chemical poisoning than adults are. Children in the womb are the most vulnerable of all. I hope that someday our environment will be so clean that all our children will be "above average."

AND NOW FOR SOME REALLY SOBERING NEWS

In a study published in 1992, Richard Peterson of the University of Wisconsin School of Pharmacy found that a single dose of dioxin given to pregnant rats damaged the reproductive systems of their pups. The lowest doses of dioxin tested were very close to the levels of dioxins and related compounds found in humans in the United States, Japan, and other industrialized countries.

Ornithologists have observed that fish-eating birds whose fishy diet contains high levels of PCBs and dioxins are sadly lacking in parental skills compared to uncontaminated birds. The PCB-exposed birds are less inclined to incubate or defend their eggs, and have a deplorable tendency to abandon their nests, leaving their defenseless eggs to the tender mercies of predators.

Anthropologist Elizabeth Guillette, of the University of Arizona at Tucson, studied Yaqui Indian children in the agricultural Yaqui Valley in Mexico to determine the effects of heavy pesticide exposures on their development.

Farming in the Yaqui Valley is mechanized, irrigated, chemically fertilized, and loaded with pesticides. Valley farmers plant up to two crops per year; each crop can have up to forty-five pesticide applications. Household bug sprays are used every day in lowland homes.

Children from the nearby foothills, where ranching is the main business, were used as the control group—matched by age and gender with the valley children. All of the foothill families with eligible children agreed to participate in the study, while 10 percent of the valley families with eligible children refused to participate in the study. In the valley, according to Guillette, "fathers were most likely to deny permission. With discussion, they admitted that they suspected pesticides were harmful for children and did not want to know about their specific child."

Guillette's tests showed that the pesticide-exposed valley children had much poorer memories, poorer hand-eye coordination, and far less endurance than their uncontaminated foothill peers. In watching the children play, Guillette noticed that the valley children were more aggressive and less creative than the foothill children.

As part of the test, the researchers asked the children to draw a person. Some of their drawings are reproduced on page 119.

Representative drawings of a person by Yaqui children from the valley and foothills of Sonora, Mexico.

Some scientists estimate that at least 5 percent of babies in the U.S. are exposed to levels of PCBs sufficient to cause neurological impairment.

> *Have the chemical manufacturers eaten too much of their own product?*
>
> *There are over 100,000 chemicals now on the market. One thousand new chemicals are made every year. Worldwide, there is enough capability to test five hundred chemicals per year. At present, no chemicals are being tested for hormonal effects before they are released on the market.*

An estimated 5 to 10 percent of school-age children in the U.S. have attention deficit disorder (ADD) or hyperactivity. Coincidence?

All over the world, poor people are the most likely to be poisoned by hazardous substances, since hazardous facilities are almost always located in poor neighborhoods. The factory explosion in Bhopal, India, which released toxic clouds of methyl isocyanate (used in making pesticides), could never have happened in Palm Springs. The people maimed and killed by the explosion were too poor even to buy the products of the factory.

Demand that your local stores carry nontoxic products.

Sick or undernourished people are also less able to ward off the effects of exposure to dangerous chemicals than are better-fed people.

In the U.S., migrant farmworkers are exposed to higher levels of toxins than the rest of us can even imagine. Many of these farmworkers are children.

Even if you are not a farmworker, your children may be exposed to higher levels of pesticides than are acceptable. The Consumers Union recently analyzed data from the U.S. Department of Agriculture that were the results of testing done on 27,000 five-pound samples of produce. Twenty-seven categories of food were tested between 1994 and 1997. The Consumers Union reported that in 1996, two out of five U.S.-grown peaches contained levels of methyl parathion that were so high that a single peach exceeded the EPA's current safe daily limit for the average 44-pound five-year-old.

Methyl parathion is one of the most potent of the organophosphate insecticides. "Organophosphates are all designed to be neurological poisons," said Dr. Philip Landrigan, of Mount Sinai School of Medicine in New York. "They work fundamentally the same in humans as in insects."

The USDA found aldicarb, an acutely toxic pesticide, in about 6 percent of the potatoes tested in 1997. About one in twenty of these potatoes exceeded the safe limit for a young child.

Try to encourage organic farmers by buying organic food whenever you can afford to—it costs more at the checkout counter, but consider the difference in price to be a donation toward improving the health of all of our children.

Organic groceries!

IN CONCLUSION

IT IS THE DUTY of all of us adults to pass this world on to our children in better shape than it was when we entered it. We must never forget or lose sight of that fact.

I hope that if you come away with anything at all from this book, it is the idea that gardening is supposed to be fun, not a struggle. We inhabitants of rich, industrialized countries are very lucky. I am not in danger of starving to death if my garden fails, and probably, gentle reader, neither are you.

Though gardening is no longer a physical necessity for most of us, it is a spiritual necessity for many of us. Sharing my garden with other animals, vertebrate and invertebrate, is one of the great pleasures of my life.

Sometimes I even enjoy the pleasure of invertebrates in the comfort of my own home. One of my favorite summers was the one we named "the beetle summer" because a dozen predatory darkling beetles bivouacked in our house. All summer long we happily watched our small, iridescent black pets as they trundled across the floor in search of invertebrate prey, and heard the occasional "beetle in distress" rustling around in a wastebasket, waiting to be liberated.

Try some of the methods in this book, then invent some of your own. Converse with your friends, neighbors, and relatives about nontoxic pest control; they may have some really fun recipes to share with you, and anecdotes about your pest control experiments are sure to thrill distinguished dinner guests!

All there! Thank God!

BIBLIOGRAPHY

I HAVE READ A great many books on gardening and agriculture, and I have found that many of the older books, which were written pre–World War II, are more satisfying to read than some of the newer books. Before World War II, chemical agriculture was very rare, and the agricultural pioneers who developed new techniques and wrote about them tended to be interesting writers.

The following list includes some of my favorite gardening and agriculture books, as well as all of the home hints books I used in writing *Slug Bread & Beheaded Thistles*.

America's Neighborhood Bats. Merlin D. Tuttle. Austin: University of Texas Press, 1988. (Bat-house building and bat-exclusion information from America's favorite Bat Man)

The Audubon Society Field Guide to North American Insects & Spiders. Lorus and Margery Milne. New York: Alfred A. Knopf, 1980. (Before you squish, identify.)

The Audubon Society Field Guide to North American Mammals. John O. Whitaker, Jr. New York: Alfred A. Knopf, 1980.

The Audubon Society Field Guide to North American Reptiles and Amphibians. John L. Behler and F. Wayne King. New York: Alfred A. Knopf, 1979.

The Best of the Hardiest. John J. Sabuco. Flossmoor, Ill.: Good Earth Publishing, Ltd., 1985. (The best book for information on choosing truly cold-hardy trees, shrubs, and perennials)

The Bug Book. Helen and John Philbrick. Pownal, Vt.: Garden Way Publishing, 1974.

Dan's Practical Guide to Least Toxic Home Pest Control. Dan Stein. Eugene, Ore.: Hulogosi, 1991.

Don Aslett's Stainbuster's Bible; The Complete Guide to Spot Removal. Don Aslett. New York: A Plumebook, Penguin Group, 1990.

Gardening for a Greener Planet; A Chemical-Free Approach. Jonathon Erickson. Blue Ridge Summit, Pa.: Tab Books, 1992.

Gardening Without Poisons. Beatrice Trum Hunter. Boston: Houghton Mifflin Company, 1971.

Handbook of Toxic and Hazardous Chemicals and Carcinogens, 3rd ed. Marshall Sittig. Westwood, N.J.: Noyes Data Corp., 1991.

Heloise Hints for a Healthy Planet. Heloise Cruse. New York: Perigee Books, The Putnam Publishing Group, 1990.

Household Ecology. Julia Percivall and Pixie Burger. Englewood Cliffs, N.J.: Prentice-Hall, 1971.

The How and Why of Better Gardening. Laurence Manning. New York: Van Nostrand Reinhold Company, Inc., 1953. (A classic old book of botany for gardeners)

How Do I Clean the Moosehead? Don Aslett. New York: New American Library, 1989. (Don Aslett runs a large cleaning business, and is the most businesslike of all the cleaning authors.)

How to Do Almost Everything. Bert Bacharach, Sr. New York: Simon and Schuster, 1970.

How to Grow Fresh Air; 50 Houseplants that Purify Your Home or Office. Dr. B. C. Wolverton. New York: Penguin Books, 1997.

The Humane Control of Wildlife in Cities and Towns. The Humane Society of the United States. Helena, Mont.: Falcon Press, 1991.

The Insect Guide. Ralph B. Swain, Ph.D. Garden City, N.Y.: The Country Life Press, 1948.

Mary Ellen's Best of Helpful Hints. Pearl Higgenbotham and Mary Ellen Pinkham. New York: Warner Books, Inc., 1979.

The Natural Formula Book for Home and Yard. Dan Wallace, editor. Emmaus, Pa.: Rodale Press, 1982.

1999 Physicians' Desk Reference. Montvale, N.J.: Medical Economics Company.

The No Work Garden Book. Ruth Stout. Emmaus, Pa.: Rodale Press, 1971. (Ruth Stout pioneered the technique of mulching gardens very heavily.)

Old Wives' Lore for Gardeners. Maureen and Bridget Boland. New York: Farrar, Straus and Giroux, 1976.

One Man's Meat. E. B. White. (Originally published in 1938 by Harper and Row; now published by Tilbury House, Gardiner, Me.).

Organic Plant Protection. Roger B. Yepson, Jr., editor. Emmaus, Pa.: Rodale Press, 1976.

Our Stolen Future. Theo Colburn. New York: Penguin Books USA, copyright 1996, Theo Colburn, Dianne Dumanski, and John Peterson Myers.

Paint Your House with Powdered Milk. Joey Green. New York: Hyperion, 1996.

Plowman's Folly. Edward H. Faulkner. New York: Grosset and Dunlap, 1943.

Polish Your Furniture with Pantyhose. Joey Green. New York: Hyperion, 1995.

Rodale's Chemical-Free Yard and Garden. A. Carr, F. M. Bradley, F. Marshall, eds. Emmaus, Pa.: Rodale Press, 1991.

Rodale's Garden Problem Solver; Vegetables, Fruits and Herbs. Jeff Ball. Emmaus, Pa.: Rodale Press, 1988.

Save Time, Save Money, Save Yourself. Dorsey Connors. New York: Hawthorne Books, Inc., 1972.

Suzanne's Garden Secrets. Suzanne Warner Pierot. Indianapolis: Bobbs-Merrill, 1978.

Systematic Dictionary of Mammals of the World. Maurice Burton. New York: Thomas Y. Crowell Company, 1962.

Tiny Game Hunting: Environmentally Healthy Ways to Trap and Kill the Pests in Your House and Garden. Hilary Dole Klein and Adrian M. Wenner. New York: Bantam Books, 1991. (This book is wonderful: the best pest control book I have ever seen. Mr. Wenner is a zoologist and really knows his stuff.)

Weeds and What They Tell. Ehrenfried E. Pfeiffer. Springfield, Ill.: Bio-Dynamic Literature, 1974. (Analyzing soil based on the "weeds" growing in it)

Works and Days, Hesiod, translated by David Grene, in *God and the Land,* Stephanie A. Nelson, Oxford University Press, 1998. (Hesiod wrote about farming before the ancient Greeks even knew they were Greeks.)

Yankee Home Hints. Earl Proulx. Emmaus, Pa.: Yankee Books, Rodale Press, 1993.

BACKGROUND INFORMATION

Alice in Wonderland, Lewis Carroll.

archie and mehitabel, Don Marquis, Doubleday, 1950.

Chaos, James Gleick, Penguin, 1988.

Chemical Deception; The Toxic Threat to Health and the Environment, Marc Lappe, Ph.D., Sierra Club, 1992.

Common Weeds of the United States, U.S. Department of Agriculture, Dover Publications, Inc, 1971.

Epitaphs, Frederic W. Unger, The Penn Publishing Company, 1904.

The Formation of Vegetable Mould Through the Action of Earthworms, With Observations on Their Habits, Charles Darwin.

The Masks of God., 4 volumes: *Primitive Mythology, 1959; Oriental Mythology, 1962; Occidental Mythology, 1964; Creative Mythology, 1968,* Joseph Campbell, Penguin Books, 1962.

New Larousse Encyclopedia of Mythology, intro by Robert Graves. The Hamlyn Publishing Group, Limited New Edition, 1968.

The One-Straw Revolution, Masanobu Fukuoka, Rodale Press, 1978.

Our Plundered Planet, Fairfield Osborn, Little, Brown, 1948.

The Religions of Man, Huston Smith, Harper and Row, 1958.

Toxicology: A Primer, Michael A. Kamrin, Ph.D., Lewis Publishers, 1988.

Weeds, Guardians of the Soil, Joseph A. Cocannouer, Devin-Adair, 1950.

Wild Animals of North America, National Geographic Society, 1987.

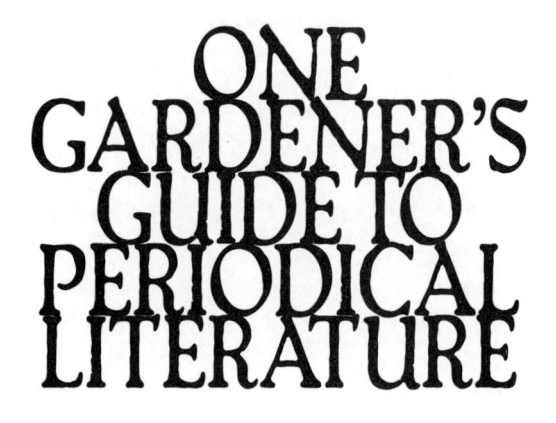

ONE GARDENER'S GUIDE TO PERIODICAL LITERATURE

Magazines and journals can help keep you up-to-date on the latest discoveries. This book could not have been written at all without information from the following wonderful publications:

Country Journal
P.O. Box 392
Mt. Morris, IL 61054

Countryside and Small Stock Journal
Countryside
W11564 Highway 64
Withee, WI 54498

Environmental Health Perspectives; Journal of the National Institute of Health Sciences
U.S. Department of Health and Human Services
U.S. Government Information
P.O. Box 371954
Pittsburgh, PA 15250-7954

Harrowsmith Country Life
Telemedia Communications, U.S.A. Inc.

Ferry Road
Charlotte, VT 05445
(Since I first published *Slug Bread,* Harrowsmith has ceased
publication.)

National Gardening, The National Gardening Association
magazine
180 Flynn Avenue
Burlington, VT 05401

Organic Gardening
Rodale Press
33 East Minor St.
Emmaus, PA 18098-0099

Pomona: The Journal of the North American Fruit Explorers
Jill Vorbeck
Route 1, Box 94
Chapin, IL 62628
www.nafex.org

Science News: The Weekly Newsmagazine of Science
1719 N Street, N.W.,
Washington, DC 20036

SOURCES FOR ORGANIC NECESSITIES OF HOME AND GARDEN LIFE

ORGANIC FERTILIZERS, PESTICIDES, AND SUPPLIES

Gardener's Supply Company
128 Intervale Road
Burlington, VT 05401-2850

Gardens Alive!
5100 Schenley Place
Lawrenceburg, IN 47025

HOUSEHOLD AND CLEANING SUPPLIES

Real Goods
200 Clara Ave.
Ukiah, CA 95482-3471

The Vermont Country Store
P.O. Box 3000
Manchester Ctr., VT 05255-3000

Permissions

The following publishers have generously granted permission to use quotations from the copyrighted works:

"pity the poor spiders" from *archy and mehitabel* by Don Marquis. Used by permission of Doubleday.

"Hot Weather" and "A Winter Diary" from *One Man's Meat* by E. B. White. Copyright © 1944 by E. B. White. Published by Tilbury House Publishers. Used by permission.

Toxicology: A Primer by Michael A. Kamrin. 1988, Lewis Publishers, a subsidiary of CRC Press, Boca Raton, Florida. Used by permission.

Paragraph on Lindane reprinted by permission from the 1999 *Physicians' Desk Reference* 53rd Edition, Medical Economics, Inc., Montvale, N.J. 07645-1742.

"Works and Days" by Hesiod trans. David Grene, from *God and the Land: The Metaphysics of Farming in Hesiod and Virgil* by Stephanie Nelson. Copyright © 1998 by Oxford University Press, Inc. Used by permission of Oxford University Press, Inc.

INDEX